BREAKING THE MOULD

SCULPTURE BY WOMEN SINCE 1945

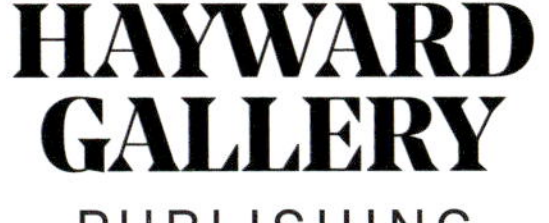

HAYWARD GALLERY PUBLISHING

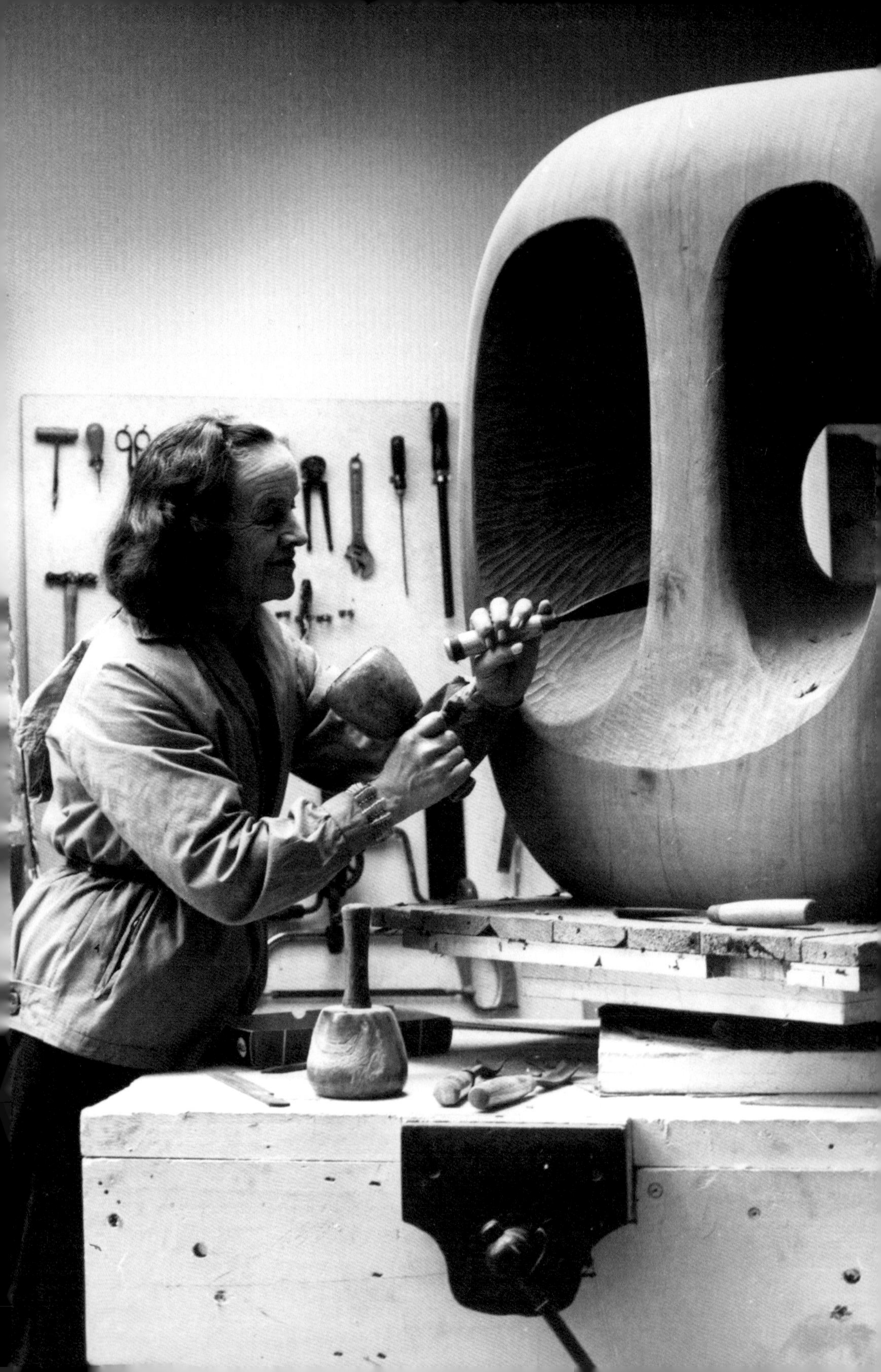

FOREWORD

There is much to be excited about in terms of the Arts Council Collection's recent investment in sculpture by women. In the last 20 years the Collection has acquired a diverse range of sculpture by Rana Begum, Karla Black, Alice Channer, Anthea Hamilton, Holly Hendry, Goshka Macuga, Heather Phillipson, Eva Rothschild and Rebecca Warren among many others, and has lent these important acquisitions to venues and exhibitions across the UK and internationally. External funds are increasingly required to support the purchase of major works by artists including Phyllida Barlow and Helen Marten, reflecting the growing market value of art by women. Where possible, steps have been taken to address 'gaps' in earlier holdings, through the retrospective investment in works by artists including Shelagh Cluett, Gillian Lowndes and Margaret Organ. However, in the acquisition period 2017–18, the Collection invested in the work of more women than men for the first time in its history, and, during the period 2018–19 all of the external acquisition committee members were female, marking a significant step forward. It is always important to maintain an objective view. For example, the Arts Council Collection did not acquire work by Phyllida Barlow until 2016, despite her longstanding contribution to British art. Furthermore, when one looks back across the Collection's long history, it is clear that sculpture by women has not been supported consistently.

It was from this intriguing position of success and shortfall that the idea for an exhibition exploring sculpture by women first began to emerge. In 2016, Dr Catherine George, now at Coventry University, and the independent curator Hilary Gresty contacted our Senior Curator Natalie Rudd to tell us about their research project, *Women Working in Sculpture from 1960 to the Present Day: Towards a New Lexicon*. Initially supported by funding from the Henry Moore Foundation, this collaborative project involved extensive interviews with sculptors with the aim of shedding fresh light on the experiences and contributions made by women to the field of modern and contemporary sculpture. Through conversation, it became clear that the Collection's holdings would provide an outstanding context from which to develop an exhibition on this subject. We remain very

grateful to Catherine and Hilary for their willingness to allow their
research to act as a catalyst for further thinking and programming.
Our thanks also go to Professor Joy Sleeman at the Slade School of
Fine Art for her ongoing support.

A spirit of dialogue has informed the curation of *Breaking
the Mould: Sculpture by Women since 1945*. Natalie Rudd and Laura
Biddle, Collection Coordinator, have worked closely with our tour
partners to create an exhibition intended to resonate across
locations and venues. I am deeply grateful to Natalie for her
dedication and drive in developing this project, and her excellent
catalogue essay. Our appreciation must also go to Laura Biddle
for the fantastic curatorial support she has provided throughout.
Special thanks are due to Deborah Robinson and Hannah Anderson
at The New Art Gallery Walsall; Neil Walker at Djanogly Art Gallery,
Lakeside Arts, University of Nottingham; Claire Longrigg, Sam
Metz and Leonie O'Dwyer at Ferens Art Gallery Hull; and Dr Sarah
Chapman at The Levinsky Gallery, The Arts Institute, University
of Plymouth: their ideas and contributions have helped mould the
exhibition into great shape. We are delighted that Angelica Vanasse
has developed an innovative suite of interpretation materials to
tour as part of the exhibition, ensuring relevance and prompting
further conversations.

An exhibition of this scale can only be realised through
the hard work and commitment of many colleagues. I would like
to thank the Sculpture Technicians, Richard Morrow and David
Willett, for their attention to all technical aspects, and Zoe Carlon,
Collection Assistant, for her excellent administrative support. My
gratitude extends to former team members, Emii Alrai, Rachel
Graves and Bhavisha Kukadia-Moran, for their work at an earlier
stage. Rob Hill and Heather Welsh have made an invaluable
contribution to communications and digital resources, ably assisted
by Grace Beaumont. The driver-technical team continues to provide
outstanding practical support, and special mention also goes to
Alison Maun and Imogen Winter.

Breaking the Mould: Sculpture by Women since 1945 is the
first survey of post-war British sculpture by women. Therefore, it
has felt important to secure a published outcome, highlighting
legacies and signposting future potential directions. We are very
grateful to Alice Nightingale and her colleagues in the Hayward
Gallery Publishing team, Diana Adell and Alex Glen, for producing

this informative and engaging book, which has been beautifully designed by the collaborative partnership Narrate + Kelly Barrow. Sincerest thanks go to all of the artists, writers and curators who have contributed a text to this volume, taking time out from busy schedules to share reflections, experiences and ideas with much generosity and thoughtfulness.

Of course, the greatest acknowledgement must be reserved for the many women who have produced outstanding examples of sculpture across the years, sometimes in the face of significant obstacles and derision. It is with regret that we have been unable to include all artists represented by the Arts Council Collection in this exhibition, but it is hoped that greater consciousness will lead to increased visibility going forward. The Arts Council Collection is much richer for their contributions and this book is dedicated to them.

JILL CONSTANTINE
DIRECTOR, ARTS COUNCIL COLLECTION

NATALIE
RUDD

KEEPING WATCH

EXPANDING THE NARRATIVES OF MODERN BRITISH SCULPTURE

The first work by a sculptor ever to be purchased for the Arts Council Collection was a drawing by Barbara Hepworth. *Reconstruction* p. 26 (1947) is one of around 80 works on paper made by the artist in response to an invitation from the surgeon Norman Capener to observe the intricate procedures of an operating theatre. Hepworth had met Capener some years earlier when he had operated on her daughter, Sarah. *Reconstruction* depicts a huddle of clinicians absorbed in the painstaking art of surgery. The scene is surprisingly sculptural, with precision tools and purposeful hands constructing an abstract form in space. Towards the left of the drawing, a female figure maintains an active gaze. Does she represent the mother, anguished at her sick child? Is she a member of the team, part of the collective endeavour? Or, does her relative distance perhaps suggest dissatisfaction – possibly a reflection of Hepworth's experience of working within the 'male occupation' of sculpture?[1] The decision by the Arts Council to purchase a work by Barbara Hepworth just one year after the establishment of the Collection reflects her position as a leading British sculptor of international repute. However, the choice of a drawing rather than a three-dimensional work highlights the tentative position of a loan collection in its infancy, taking first steps towards the acquisition of sculpture.[2] Since the purchase of *Reconstruction*, the Arts Council Collection has acquired more than 1000 sculptures and installations, more than 250 of which were created by women.

The enquiry into the contribution made by women working within the field of modern and contemporary British sculpture has still to be fully established. *Breaking the Mould: Sculpture by Women since 1945* takes a first step towards a greater understanding of this subject. Operating on the principle of a 'curatorial corrective'[3] and using the rich holdings of the Arts Council Collection as its starting point, the exhibition places sculpture by women front and centre. This radical recalibration provides a riposte to the many surveys of British sculpture that have marginalised women or airbrushed their work from the story altogether.[4] The aim of this essay is to outline the cultural context, highlighting some of the long-held assumptions about women working in sculpture and revealing various strategies undertaken by individuals and groups to break new ground. Where possible, reference will be made to artists' statements to convey first-hand experiences across time. It is also important to acknowledge the concurrent interrogation across society of static definitions of gender and the need to improve representation of work by artists identifying as non-binary. *Breaking the Mould* advocates for a sustained collective endeavour to increase representation within the discourses of sculpture.

A MALE OCCUPATION

In 1966, the art critic Robert Hughes interviewed Barbara Hepworth at her St Ives studio. He was instantly struck by her petite stature: 'How could this diminutive woman, 62 years old, with skin and flesh laid over bones as delicate as a seagull's, have modelled and carved a body of work five times the size of Michelangelo's in equally resistant materials and on as big a scale?' Hepworth's response was robust: 'I am constantly plagued by this little woman attitude.' She continued: 'There is a deep prejudice against women in art. Many people – most people still, I imagine – think that women should not involve themselves in the act of creation except on its more trivial fringes. They still think of sculpture as a male occupation: because, I suppose, they have a misconception of what sculpture involves. There is this cliché, you see, a sculptor is a muscular brute bashing at an inert lump of stone, but sculpture is not rape. No good form is hacked. Stone never surrenders to force.'[5]

A similar preoccupation with physical appearance infuses many written assessments of Elisabeth Frink's work. Frink, a significant figure in post-war British sculpture, well known for her expressive representations of animals, birds and male figures, tended to work in plaster before casting her work in bronze. In his 'official' biography, Stephen Gardiner discussed Frink's appearance at various points, as in this passage where he reflects on how 'she had a somewhat masculine appearance; accompanying broad shoulders and narrow hips [...] A Renaissance look about her graceful strong hands, a high forehead, pronounced Roman nose, a Greek touch in her neatly shaped mouth.'[6] One senses a difficulty among male critics in believing that a female could produce work of this quality, leading to an overreliance on the idea that there must be something of the male about her. In response to a similar line of enquiry in an interview with the curator and art historian Norman Rosenthal, Frink's provides swift clarification: 'I am not androgynous.'[7]

Unlike many of their female contemporaries, both Hepworth and Frink experienced high levels of recognition during their lifetimes, as evidenced in the Arts Council Collection's prompt investment in their work. The Arts Council purchased Frink's *Bird* (1952) at a very early stage in her career – in 1953, the same year that she graduated from Chelsea School of Art. Nevertheless, although the Collection holds five works by Hepworth and six by Frink, Henry Moore is represented by 13 drawings and 11 sculptures.[8] The monolithic status of Moore dominated the post-war years. Hepworth's proximity to Moore – just a few years younger, raised and educated in West Yorkshire, occupying the same artistic circles and sharing some sculptural concerns – led to frequent comparisons. Critics perceived her work to be derivative, that of a disciple rather than an equal. Hepworth struggled to find committed advocacy from Herbert Read, the eminent critic and champion of post-war British sculpture. While he commented extensively on Moore's genius, Read's output on Hepworth is notable for its muted ambivalence, evidenced in his frequent deferral to her own statements rather than taking the trouble to engage in fresh analysis.[9]

With the myth of the male sculptor deeply ingrained in the processes and discourses of post-war British sculpture, it is of little surprise to learn that a large proportion of the women who succeeded in having their sculpture acquired by the Arts Council Collection during the 1950s and 1960s had a strong connection with a male sculptor or influencer, usually through marriage. Mentioning this is not to denigrate the quality of their work but rather to highlight the additional means and connections needed for a woman to be recognised. Karin Jonzen, whose terracotta *Seated Nude* was the p. 27 first sculpture by a woman to be purchased for the collection in 1951, was married to the painter and art collector Basil Jonzen. Together, they established a commercial art gallery which attracted many notable collectors. Anthea Alley is represented in the collection by two works: *Horse* (1960) and *Rock* (1964). Alley was married p. 55 to the art historian and Tate Gallery curator, Ronald Alley: they entertained many art world friends in their London home. Rosemary Young studied at the Slade School of Fine Art from 1949. Here she was taught by the sculptor Reg Butler. They formed a relationship and later married, having two children together. Despite early success in the mid 1950s with figurative works such as *Girl Drying* p. 68 *Her Foot*, Young was soon fully committed to supporting Butler with his work, leaving little time or mental space to pursue her own ideas: 'there was always a demand on me to, to help […] he [Reg] couldn't

work with assistants [...] I'm the only person that's ever worked with
him [...] I was in an incredibly privileged position, to be able to be that
person. But it became [...] my role. So there was no space to suddenly
say, "I'm going to make a sculpture" [...] And anyway, it had gone, it
had just disappeared.' [10]

THE SCULPTURE DEPARTMENT

The 'macho' domain of sculpture departments in British art
schools requires a section of its own, so prevalent are the accounts
of endemic sexism experienced by women during their time there.
A number of these anecdotes reference Reg Butler. In 1961, Butler
delivered a series of five lectures to students at the Slade, which
were later published. In one lecture, he set out his views of female
art students: 'I am quite sure the vitality of a great many female
students derives from frustrated maternity, and most of these, on
finding the opportunity to settle down and produce children, will
no longer experience a degree of passionate discontent sufficient to
drive them constantly towards the labours of creation in other ways.' [11]
Phyllida Barlow recalls an encounter with Butler on her first day at
the Slade in 1963: 'He said, "because you are a woman, I'm not that
interested, because by the time you're 30 you will be having babies
and making jam. And [...] apart from Barbara [Hepworth] [...] Name
a woman sculptor [...] Let me tell you, there are none." [...] I remember
meeting George Fullard after [...] my first year at the Slade, and he
said, "What's it been like?" and I said, "Absolutely awful." [...] And
then I told him the story about Reg Butler, and I remember George
saying, "What he doesn't realise is that women will actually be the
major artistic [...] drive in a few years [...] He doesn't understand the
notion of a female creativity, and the number of men who also have
to use the female side of themselves to, to make art"'. [12]
    Much has been written about Anthony Caro's transformation
of the sculpture department at St Martin's School of Art during the
1950s and 1960s. Following a 1959 trip to the United States, Caro
moved away from gestural representations of the female form and
towards purely abstract sculpture, welded from steel, placed directly
on the floor and painted in a rainbow of colours. Inspired by his
conversations with the critic and theorist Clement Greenberg, Caro
set about transforming the studio spaces at St Martin's into sites
for critical discussion, or, as the artist Bruce McLean recalls from

his student days: 'Twelve adult men with pipes would walk for hours around sculpture and mumble.'[13] The criticism could be brutal, with students expected to deliver strong verbal defences. Kim Lim, who had moved from Singapore to London at the age of 18 to study sculpture at St Martin's, recalled that Caro was 'very different from the kind of teachers I've had [...] very confrontational, which was meant to draw people out and be challenging, which is very good [...] But at the time I wasn't ready for that, because having come from a society where you listened and you never answered back or were asked to think, I found that quite frightening and difficult.'[14] The sculptor Wendy Taylor considered herself 'tough', having been raised in the East End of London, but she found that she needed all her resilience to cut through the prejudice at St Martin's (1961–67). 'I was the only female in my year – it was hell', she reflected recently, remembering the reluctance of her tutors to accept her on their class lists and warning her not to use up all the tools and materials.[15]

Ironically too, despite also showing a territorial hostility and unwillingness to share, Taylor's male contemporaries did not hold back in coating their sculptures in colours more often associated with the 'feminine' domain of cosmetics. A striking feature of the sculpture produced by the so-called 'New Generation' of artists working in direct response to Caro, was the emergence of smooth, sensual surfaces licked with shades of puce, powder pink, lipstick red.

Adopting 'feminine' materials and techniques was a deliberate strategy used by the American artist Jann Haworth, who moved to London from California in 1961 to study at the Slade: 'The assumption was that, as one tutor put it, "the girls were there to keep the boys happy." He prefaced that by saying "it wasn't necessary for them to look at the portfolios of the female students... they just needed to look at their photos." From that point, it was head-on competition with the male students. I was annoyed enough, and American enough, to take that on. I was determined to better them, and that's one of the reasons for the partly sarcastic choice of cloth, latex and sequins as media. It was a female language to which the male students didn't have access.'[16] Taking its title from the favourite flower of the artist's mother, *Calendula's Cloak* (1967) p. 29 is an excellent example of Haworth's unique body of work. This life-size female figure emerges from a process of stitching together a soft patchwork of brightly coloured scraps of patterned fabric. Intentionally homespun and handcrafted, Haworth's work proposed a radically different approach to sculpture, one driven by subjective female experience and resulting in a soft and tactile figuration. Margaret Organ, studying at the art department at Brighton Polytechnic during the mid 1970s, became disheartened by the lack of role models. She quickly acknowledged her disinterest in welding heavy materials and conforming to male preconceptions of sculpture. Instead, Organ began to experiment with paper and cotton, working by hand to create softer, flowing, organic forms,

p. 85 of which *Loop* (1978/2014), is a fine example. Organ reflected some years later that 'gentleness in sculpture is invariably far stronger than the aggressive facade of work which has an overt strength.'[17] Organ drew inspiration from the German-born American sculptor Eva Hesse, who achieved international recognition during the 1960s for sculptures and installations that employed a vast range of materials including latex, cloth, rope, plastic and mesh. Hesse expanded the language of minimalism by softening its rigid geometries to create sensuous and spontaneous organic forms. Despite the freshness of Organ's contribution to a developing post-minimal language, the external assessor of her degree course found it difficult to place her work within the category of 'proper sculpture', awarding her a first-class degree with great reluctance, and only after her written contextual study of Hesse's work had been assessed.[18]

THE PRAM IN THE HALL

The writer and critic Cyril Connolly once famously stated that 'there is no more sombre enemy to good art than the pram in the hall.' This fear of mixing creativity and parenthood percolates across the decades, as evidenced in Reg Butler's aforementioned lectures and statements, and further endorsed by many subsequent artists and writers. Lingering doubts have resurfaced in recent years, as expressed in a range of recent articles investigating the challenges facing women working in the arts. In a 2013 edition of *Art Monthly*, the writer Jennifer Thatcher wrote: 'Women [...] express anxiety at the prospect of having children, feeling that they must avoid visible obstacles to their career progression in a world in which one must appear continually available for residencies, commissions or even just networking.'[19] Tracey Emin's response to the issue is characteristically forthright: 'There are good artists who have children, of course there are. They are called men.'[20] One can speak of growing awareness, the importance of multitasking and the need to build a network of support from partners, friends, families and sympathetic gallerists, but it is sobering to reflect on the 2016 survey carried out by the Office of National Statistics which discovered that women do almost 60 percent more unpaid work than men, including housework, cooking and caring.[21] Maintaining a presence in a fast-changing art scene requires time, energy and commitment – qualities that can be put under great strain when coupled with demands on the home front.

Of course, some artists become parents and others do not. Looking back at the experiences of a number of British artists with parental responsibilities, however, one is struck by an overriding sense of 'keep calm and carry on' – a necessary determination, particularly in the years before widespread childcare provision. In a frank interview with the feminist art historian Cindy Nemser, Barbara Hepworth explained: 'We lived in a world of work and the children were brought up in it, in the middle of the dust and the dirt and the paint and everything. They were just part of it[…] I mean my home came first but my work was there always.'[22]

The notion of artistic practice as just another collaborative strand of shared family life is revealed in an enlightening recollection from the painter, Sheila Girling, who was married to Anthony Caro: 'Because Tony was working in the house and in the garage, which was part of the house, I used to choose his colours. He'd got into the steel stuff then, and I would choose his colours and I would paint them by hand. I mean physically painting them[…] The baby was in the pram or[…]watching you, or staggering around […]I had lots of ideas that I could give [Tony], and he had lots of ideas to add to it, and we fed each other all the time.'[23] On a cautionary note, familial collaborations do, of course, carry the risk of leaving one party unacknowledged, as evidenced in the working partnership between Rosemary Young and Reg Butler mentioned earlier. Furthermore, it should be noted that for many women in post-war Britain, bearing new life predicated the sudden death of one's professional life, so tight was the grip of social acceptability and domestic obligation during these years. Young recalls having a wide network of fellow female students at the Slade, only to observe their gradual slippage from sight, one by one, in the years that followed.[24]

The creative potential of parenthood offers a rich source for potential future scholarship. This is an opportunity to revisit and reframe experiences often deemed to be negative and to further challenge harmful perceptions that can stoke fear. Various artists have described having experienced a surge of creativity during early parenthood, finding new ways of working during the unlikeliest of moments. As Phyllida Barlow recollects, sometimes the best ideas spring to mind in the quiet wakeful hours before dawn: 'The biggest transformation for me was perhaps having to move away from a routine that was very expansive – [before] I could begin at seven in the morning and work 'til 10 at night. With a baby, that was not possible. So I began to work at night in the dark with no lights on, and because I became so fascinated by touching and feeling a baby when you're cleaning or washing it, and all the wonderful, non-verbal contact you have with this creature, I think it got into the work in the form of a real exploration of touch. And because I turned the lights off, I was using materials in a very non-visual way.'[25]

The close physical and emotional relationship between mother and child is explored with analytical precision in Mary Kelly's six-part installation, *Post-Partum Document* (1973–79). This American-born artist moved to London in 1968 to complete her studies and became closely involved with the women's movement. *Post-Partum Document* is a seminal feminist work analysing six years of interaction between Kelly and her young son, charting their evolving relationship as he gained new skills and greater independence. To make this work, Kelly combined her knowledge of psychoanalytic theory with a museological presentation of material sourced from her experience as a mother, including soiled nappies, baby clothing and early writing samples. The resulting work brings the overlooked and unpaid work of women into the heart of intellectual discourse. Challenging the predominant view at the time that a woman's role was solely that of a caregiver, Kelly successfully established 'women's work' as a worthy source of conceptual enquiry and built a theoretical framework to prove that the roles of 'artist' and 'mother' are not mutually exclusive.

HERE TO STAY

For those artists who managed to successfully negotiate art school and to surf the social expectations of domestic responsibility, there was an additional hurdle to clear: that of maintaining visibility within a male-dominated gallery context. During a recent conference, the artist Deanna Petherbridge shared her perception of British art institutions during the 1970s, highlighting the 'strictly patriarchal controls' underpinning an 'all-powerful institutional axis' connecting the Arts Council, the British Council and the Tate Gallery. Statistical evidence of this bias can be found in a very simple analysis of the major exhibitions organised during this decade: the work of women is represented in very small percentages, if at all.[26] Given the difficulties in finding institutional footholds, many women sought opportunities elsewhere. Wendy Taylor found freedom and increased ambition in making sculpture for the public realm. No longer governed by the physical limitations of siting her sculptures in gallery spaces, she could work on a much larger scale, engaging with communities and places in more meaningful and sustained ways. Other artists circumnavigated the institutional context by realising projects in alternative spaces. This approach often led to the development of supportive networks, as the artist Rose Finn-Kelcey explained: 'I need energy from other people, other women and their work [...] Our experiences as women make us what we are and we should learn to use them and never to repress them.'[27] Working in temporary spaces often prompted a more flexible approach to materiality, as artists adapted to different contexts. Finn-Kelcey, for example, worked across sculpture, installation, film, performance and photography, and often worked collaboratively with others to produce work and to question systems of power.

During the late 1970s, the artist Liliane Lijn decided to take the issue of institutional representation by the horns. She requested a meeting with the curators at the Tate Gallery to discuss her proposal for an exhibition of work by five mid-career female artists. The proposal was flatly rejected. Following further negotiations, the Arts Council agreed to invite Lijn and her close associates, fellow artists Tess Jaray and Kim Lim, to work with Rita Donagh and Gillian Wise to curate the *Hayward Annual 1978*. This round-up of the latest trends in contemporary art had itself been the subject of much criticism, with the 1977 edition having showcased work by 29 men and just one woman. After much soul searching, the curators of the *Hayward Annual 1978* reluctantly concluded that a women-only show would be too controversial and so they opted instead for a 16:7 ratio in favour of female practice, with each artist given ample space to show a range of their work. From a contemporary perspective, the resulting exhibition appears to have been thoughtful, serious and relatively unradical; nevertheless, the shift in ratio attracted much attention, with the press dubbing the show 'Ladies' Night', 'Girls' Own Annual' and 'Wayward Gallery', with particular vitriol directed towards the feminist work of Mary Kelly.[28] Overall, Lijn and her co-curators had raised the possibility of a more inclusive approach to curating within an institutional context. By throwing 'a small cat among some large pigeons',[29] they had succeeded in opening up the debate, even if sustained change remained far on the horizon.

The struggle for visibility facing black and Asian women artists was even more acute, with artists confronted with discrimination on grounds of race as well as gender. Taking the matter into her own hands, the artist Lubaina Himid curated three landmark exhibitions in response to 'other people's urgent desire for a physical and tangible proof of our creative activity'.[30] The first two exhibitions, *Five Black Women Artists* (1983) – featuring work by Sonia Boyce, Lubaina Himid, Claudette Johnson, Houria Niati and Veronica Ryan and *Black Woman Time Now* (1983–84) – representing the work of 15 artists – took place at the Africa Centre in London, with *The Thin Black Line* opening at the Institute of Contemporary Art in 1985. This third project resulted from Himid's direct written proposal to the ICA's curator, Declan McGonagle, asking initially for 'the space, the whole space' to showcase a substantial range of work, including major presentations of sculpture by Sokari Douglas Camp and Veronica Ryan.[31] Ultimately, the area devoted to the exhibition was significantly reduced, with just an offer of the corridor space – hence the barbed linear reference of the title – and an upstairs room in which to present Ryan's work. These physical constraints did little to dampen ambitions, as evidenced in the accompanying publication: 'We are claiming what is ours and making ourselves visible. We are 11 of the hundreds of creative black women in Britain. We are here to stay.'[32]

An assessment of the purchasing decisions taken by the Arts Council Collection during the 1970s and 1980s reveals a gradual awakening on the subject of diversity and inclusion. Between 1970 and 1978, successive male purchasing committees acquired four sculptures by women and more than 75 three-dimensional works by men.[33] From 1979 there was a conscious diversification of the workforce, with more women achieving senior positions with the Arts Council and improved representation on the committee through the recruitment of female artists and curators. The impact of this change on the sculpture holdings appears to have been significant and immediate. An untitled early sculpture by Alison Wilding entered the collection in 1980, with the acquisition of Mary Kelly's work, *Post-Partum Document, Documentation VI* (1978–79), in p. 34 1981. Other important acquisitions soon followed, including early sculptures by Shirazeh Houshiary and Helen Chadwick. Investment in substantial works by Veronica Ryan and Sokari Douglas Camp followed later in the decade.[34]

SHOUT AND WHISPER

In a 2002 interview with the feminist art historian Lisa Tickner, the artist Cornelia Parker commented: 'I think we're all made up of male and female parts in our psyches and we manifest whatever, depending.'[35] Parker goes on to state: 'Sometimes you want to shout out loud, make a dramatic statement and sometimes you want to whisper.'[36] Parker's freedom to work across a range of sensibilities manifests itself in dextrous leaps, from the earth-shattering drama of an exploding shed to the forensic analysis of skin dust from Sigmund Freud's couch. A similar agility is discernible in the sculpture of Rachel Whiteread, as exemplified in *Untitled (6 Spaces)* p. 77 1994. To make this work, Whiteread cast the void spaces found beneath six domestic chairs using translucent resin. The resulting objects combine lightness and weight: at first glance these are tough, heavy forms, placed with the rhythmic pace of minimalism, yet, on closer inspection, their surfaces reveal other stories – the ethereal traces of our lives as imprinted on the worn surfaces of the objects that surround us. This powerful work prompts our recollection of both 'male' and 'female' precedents: the solid concrete cast of the space beneath Bruce Nauman's chair, for example, as well as the repeated, translucent forms of Eva Hesse's multi-part installations. In an intriguing essay, *Mediating Generation: the mother-daughter plot,* Lisa Tickner attributes this dexterity to increased access to male *and* female role models gained as a result of many years of individual and collective action by women to make and exhibit their work. Rachel Whiteread's mother, Pat, was a feminist artist, for example, and Whiteread also had the opportunity to learn from the sculptor Alison Wilding, while working as her studio assistant. As Tickner explains 'What has been won here is not a place in a separate, parallel, maternal line so much as the right to inhabit, appropriate, or "swerve" from the example of fathers and brothers as well as mothers and aunts.' [37]

For many, the sculpture produced by women during the so-called 'young British art' years is memorable for its shout rather than its whisper, notable for its headline-grabbing recourse to crude themes and for the 'unladylike' conduct of some of its protagonists. It should be acknowledged that both male and female artists engaged in unruly behaviour, reflecting, if anything, a sense of equality among the 'yBa' generation. Tracey Emin's drunk and disorderly performance on a live Channel 4 Turner Prize debate in 1997, for example, was as unsurprising as Damien Hirst's frequent devil-may-care antics: both artists provided a ready supply of entertainment for tabloid exploitation. That said, Emin's lifestyle, as evidenced through her self-reflective art, became a particular source of fascination. Her infamous tent appliquéd with the names of everyone she had ever slept with, and the unravelling narratives of her unmade bed, the site of doomed relationships and depressive bouts, left a lasting impression in the public consciousness. Sarah Lucas's sculpture involves a similar adaptation of everyday objects to address issues concerning gender, sexuality and discrimination. Bawdy humour and a playful approach to materials inform her sculptures made from stuffed tights or cigarettes, or installations in which fruit, fried eggs and kebabs are staged to suggest male and female anatomies. Figurative references abound in Anya Gallaccio's installations, which feature malleable materials such as chocolate, ice or flowers and address enduring themes of life, love, sex and
p. 63 death. *can love remember the question and the answer* (2003) features 60 red gerbera flowers encapsulated behind the glass panels of two vintage doors. Across the course of an exhibition the flowers are left to rot, shedding colour, shape and form across time. Again, the importance of many female forebears must be acknowledged, from artists exploring the potential of soft 'feminine' materials during the 1960s and 1970s, through to early feminist performance art with its political intent and confrontational physicality.

The central role of women within the art of the 1990s was highlighted by Nick Serota in 1999 as he reflected on the Turner Prize: 'In the years 1991–98 14 of the 32 nominees were women [...]

Quite suddenly, it seemed that art could be young, female and directly connected to the viewer's daily experience.'[38] Although Serota's comments reflected a growing confidence and investment in art made by women, they also prompt further reflection. Even today, only 11 women have won the Turner Prize compared with 25 male winners, and Lubaina Himid had to wait until 2017 to become the first black woman to be awarded the prize, inadvertently assuming the mantle of being the oldest winner. It should also be remembered that, beyond the household names, sculpture made by many women working during the 1990s is now at great risk of slipping out of view as the filtration processes of art history take hold.

KEEPING WATCH

An assessment of contemporary sculptural practice reveals a sense of freedom and possibility. There is widespread ambition to work across abstract and figurative modes, blurring distinctions and crossing boundaries. Rana Begum works across two and three dimensions producing intimate and meditative reliefs such as *No. 429 SFold* (2013), or creating large-scale installations for public p. 70 spaces. At first glance, Begum's work appears to occupy the realms of pure abstraction, colour and geometry, but with deeper contemplation one finds broader spheres of reference, from memories of her childhood engagement with Islamic art through to her ongoing interest in urban architecture and the repeat patterns of everyday life. Rosanne Robertson's recent sculptures, drawings and performances question fixed definitions of gender and sexuality. Acknowledging Barbara Hepworth's assertion 'I the sculptor am the landscape', Robertson has made work in direct response to the Bridestones – an outcrop of ambiguous boulder formations found on the moors near their former Yorkshire home. Through these works, Robertson questions the veracity of narrow, 'set in stone' definitions, and draws a connection between the mutability of stone, shaped by the relentless forces of water, wind and rain, and a fluid understanding of gender and sexuality.

Many artists today choose to work across media, traversing sculpture, installation and performance, digital and image-based content. Helen Marten, who won the Turner Prize and the inaugural Hepworth Prize for Sculpture in 2016, makes work that is magpie in concept and playful in meaning. *Bluebutter Idles* (2014) takes the p. 62

21

form of a visual poem: the work features a bespoke 'dumpster' filled with an intricate assortment of sourced and handmade objects. It is the responsibility of the viewer to piece together the clues, making connections and hitting dead ends, like an archaeologist assessing a find. A similar joining of seemingly disparate dots emerges in p. 69 Anthea Hamilton's work *Leg Chair (Jane Birkin)* 2011. Hamilton used her own body as the template for the laser-cut acrylic leg profiles, which are hinged to splay like an open book. This pose recalls Lewis Morley's photograph of a naked Christine Keeler sitting astride an Arne Jacobsen chair. The voluptuous chair designs of Gaetano Pesce also spring to mind, as do Allen Jones's controversial sculptures in which female mannequins are contorted to function as tables, chairs and hat stands. The addition of ephemera relating to a 1960s icon, Jane Birkin, adds another layer to Hamilton's collage of ideas concerning the representation of bodies and identities in art, design and popular culture.

In 2018 Hamilton became the first black woman to take on the commission to make new work for Tate Britain's Duveen Galleries, responding with an inventive and ambitious intervention, *The Squash*. There have been other recent institutional breakthroughs for women working in sculpture, as evidenced by the last three British Pavilion exhibitions at the Venice Biennale (Sarah Lucas in 2015, Phyllida Barlow in 2017, and Cathy Wilkes in 2019), and through a range of substantial monographic exhibitions in public spaces in recent years. That said, statistics concerning commercial representation reveal slower signs of improvement, and overall there are indicators that art by women is not entering public collections as readily as the improved exhibition representation might suggest.[39] Frances Morris, Director of Tate Modern, reflected recently that 'we really have to stop celebrating creativity depending on how it's monetised by the art market [...] It's not about constructing a collection based on shopping and taste in the private sector. We're interested in art whose value lies in excellence and provocation and fascination for the public. And, more often than not, that art is made by women.'[40]

When assessing the growing number of success stories citing improved representation, it is crucial to look and look again. As Jessica Morgan, Director of the Dia Art Foundation, cautioned recently: 'Don't accept the first story. Or even the second or the third. It is only through repeated research that you get to understand what it is you are looking at.'[41] Equally important is an acknowledgement that the historical issues raised in this text are by no means consigned to the past. The macho narratives of sculpture are persistent, eager to resurface through any available fissure. In 2019, at the end of a glowing review of an exhibition of ambitious new work by Holly Hendry, one journalist expressed her astonishment at Hendry's achievement: 'All this from a mild-mannered artist who doesn't look capable of peeling the skin off a rice pudding.'[42] A throwaway quip, perhaps, but also a stark reminder of Barbara Hepworth's long battle against 'this little woman attitude' and of the many belittling comments aimed at women working in sculpture across time. My thoughts return to the female figure in Hepworth's drawing, *Reconstruction*. She is keeping watch, fully alert.

1 For a detailed and enlightening interpretation of this drawing see Chris Stephens' illuminating essay 'From Constructivism to Reconstruction: Barbara Hepworth in the 1940s' in David Thistlewood (ed.), *Barbara Hepworth Reconsidered*, Critical Forum Series Vol. 3 (Liverpool: Liverpool University Press/Tate Gallery Liverpool, 1996), pp. 135–53

2 The first sculpture to be acquired by the Arts Council Collection was Frank Dobson's *Portrait Bust of Lady Keynes* (1924). Purchased in 1948, the work depicts the professional ballerina Lydia Lopokova, who was also the wife of John Maynard Keynes – a significant figure in the formation of the Arts Council of Great Britain

3 The term 'curatorial corrective' was used by Maura Reilly, founding curator of the Sackler Centre of Feminist Art, to describe women-only exhibitions in 'Female Artists Are (Finally) Getting Their Turn', *New York Times*, 29 March 2016, www.nytimes.com/2016/04/03/arts/design/the-resurgence-of-women-only-art-shows.html [accessed 11 February 2020]

4 The chronology on p. 104 provides a useful insight into the representation of women within prominent survey exhibitions of modern and contemporary British sculpture

5 Sarah Crompton, 'Barbara Hepworth Finally Gets Her Due', *Guardian*, 13 June 2015, www.theguardian.com/

artanddesign/2015/jun/13/barbara-hepworth-finally-gets-her-due [accessed 11 February 2020]

6   Stephen Gardiner, *Frink: The Official Biography of Elisabeth Frink* (London: HarperCollins Publishers, 1998) p. 25

7   Norman Rosenthal, interview with Elisabeth Frink, in *Elisabeth Frink: Sculpture and Drawings 1952–1984* (London: Royal Academy of Arts, 1985) p. 27

8   Henry Moore worked in an advisory capacity for the Arts Council Collection in the early years, shaping the purchases of sculpture. Letters in the Arts Council archives highlight Moore's direct advocacy of acquisitions by Frink and Hepworth

9   For an extensive analysis of the critical reception of Hepworth's work, see Katy Deepwell 'Hepworth and Her Critics', in Thistlewood (ed.), pp. 135–53

10 Rosemary Butler interviewed by Gillian Whiteley, *National Life Stories: Artists Lives*, November 1999. Bultler's interview offers a fascinating account into a life dedicated to the support of another artist

11 Reg Butler, *Creative Development: Five Lectures to Art Students* (London: Routledge and Kegan Paul, 1962), p. 11. For an interesting assessment of art school culture, see also Lisa Tickner, 'Retrospect' (2008) in Hilary Robinson, (ed.), *Feminism Art Theory: An Anthology 1968–2014* (Oxford: Blackwell Publishers, 2001), pp. 106–14

12 Phyllida Barlow interviewed by Kirstie Gregory, *National Life Stories: Artists Lives*, 2012

13 Elena Crippa, 'The Artist as a Speaker-Performer: The London Art School in the 1960s–1970s' in Jo Applin, Catherine Spencer and Amy Tobin (eds.), *London Art Worlds: Mobile, Contingent and Ephemeral Networks, 1960–1980* (Pennsylvania: Pennsylvania State University Press, 2018), p. 172. Crippa's excellent account

of the culture of St Martin's also indicates various strategies taken by women to pursue alternative ways of performing and collaborating during the 1970s

14 Michael Bird, *Studio Voices: Art and Life in Twentieth Century Britain* (London: Lund Humphries, 2018), p. 116

15 Author's conversation with Wendy Taylor, 1 October 2019

16 Interview with Jann Haworth in 'Still Swinging After All These Years?' *TATE, ETC.*, No. 1, Summer 2004, referenced in issuu.com/bloomsburypublishing/docs/iconic_design_sampler [accessed 11 February 2020]

17 Lewis Biggs, Iwona Blazwick and Sandy Nairne, Artists' statement, *Objects & Sculpture*, (London/Bristol: Institute of Contemporary Arts/Arnolfini, 1981), p. 24

18 Author's conversation with Margaret Organ, 19 June 2019

19 Jennifer Thatcher, '50:50', *Art Monthly*, No. 367, June 2013, pp. 5–8

20 Anna Brady, 'Bringing Up Baby: Making Motherhood Work in the Art World', *Art Newspaper*, 12 June 2019, www.theartnewspaper.com/feature/bringing-up-baby-making-motherhood-work-in-the-art-world [accessed 10 February 2020]

21 See Oliver Burkeman, 'Dirty Secret: Why is There Still a Gender Housework Gap?', *Guardian*, 20 February 2018, www.theguardian.com/inequality/2018/feb/17/dirty-secret-why-housework-gender-gap [accessed 11 February 2020]

22 Cindy Nemser, *Art Talk: Conversations with 12 Women Artists* (New York: Charles Scribner's Sons, 1975), p. 14

23 Bird, p. 43

24 Butler interviewed by Whiteley, 1999

25 Phyllida Barlow and Anna Maria Maiolino, 'In Conversation: Art Politics, Motherhood', *New York Times Style Magazine*, 28 November 2018, p. 3

26 Petherbridge was speaking at the symposium, 'The Hayward Annual Exhibition 1978 Revisited', at the Henry Moore Institute, 12 December 2018. See the Chronology for further data regarding the gender bias of exhibitions; it should be noted that such skewed statistics continue well beyond the 1970s

27 Sarah Kent, 'Engendering Self-Respect', *Studio International*, Vol. 193, No. 987/3, May/June 1977, p. 196. This special edition focused exclusively on art by women and offered valuable insights into the challenges and opportunities experienced by artists during this time

28 For an in-depth analysis of reactions to this exhibition, see Griselda Pollock, 'Feminism, Femininity and the Hayward Annual Exhibition 1978', *Feminist Review*, Vol. 2, No. 1, July 1979, p. 33–55

29 Tess Jaray, artist's statement read at the symposium, 'The Hayward Annual Exhibition 1978 Revisited'

30 Lubaina Himid, *Thin Black Line(s)*, a Making Histories Visible project, exhibited at University of Central Lancashire, Tate Britain and UCLAN, 2011–12, p. 10, clok.uclan.ac.uk/5106/22/thinblacklinesbook.pdf [accessed 11 February 2020]

31 Himid, p.26

32 Eddie Chambers, *Black Artists in British Art: A History since the 1950s* (London: I.B. Tauris, 2014), p. 131

33 Angela Conner, *Lord Goodman* (1972, purchased 1972); Katherine Gili, *Vertical III* (1975, purchased 1975); Liliane Lijn, *See Thru Koan* (1969, purchased 1975); Wendy Taylor, *Inversion* (1970, purchased 1970)

34 See Dr Anjalie Dalal-Clayton's 2018 report *National Collections Audit, Black Artists & Modernism*. Although Arts Council Collection tops the list of major UK collections in terms of having the largest number of black artists represented in its holdings, 94 out of more than 2000 artists still marks a relatively small percentage of the overall collection

35 'A Strange Alchemy: Cornelia Parker interviewed by Lisa Tickner', in Gill Perry (ed.), *Difference and Excess in Contemporary Art: The Visibility of Women's Practice* (Oxford: Blackwell Publishing, 2004), p. 50

36 Parker interviewed by Tickner, p. 68

37 Lisa Tickner, 'Mediating Generation: the mother-daughter plot', *Art History*, Vol. 25, No. 1, February 2002, p. 30

38 Parker interviewed by Tickner, p. 13

39 Charlotte Burns and Julia Halperin, 'Museums Claim They're Paying More Attention to Female Artists. That's an Illusion', *artnet*, 19 September 2019, news.artnet.com/womens-place-in-the-art-world/womens-place-art-world-museums-1654714 [accessed 10 February 2020]

40 Hannah Ellis-Peterson, 'How the Art World Airbrushed Female Artists from History', *Guardian*, 6 February 2017, www.theguardian.com/lifeandstyle/2017/feb/06/how-the-art-world-airbrushed-female-artists-from-history [accessed 10 February 2020]

41 Ibid, footnote 39

42 Harriet Lloyd-Smith, 'Junk Rocker: Artist Holly Hendry's New Solo Show Conveys Her Taste for Waste', *Wallpaper**, No. 247, October 2019, www.wallpaper.com/art/holly-hendry-yorkshire-sculpture-park [accessed 10 February 2020]

BARBARA
HEPWORTH

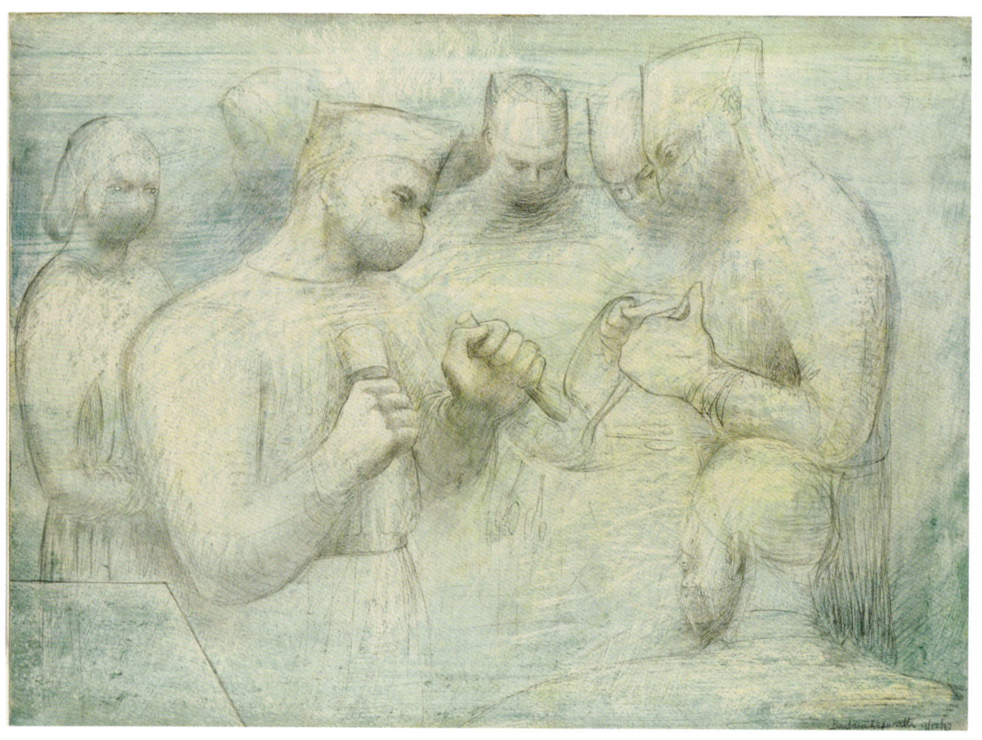

Reconstruction, 1947

KARIN
JONZEN

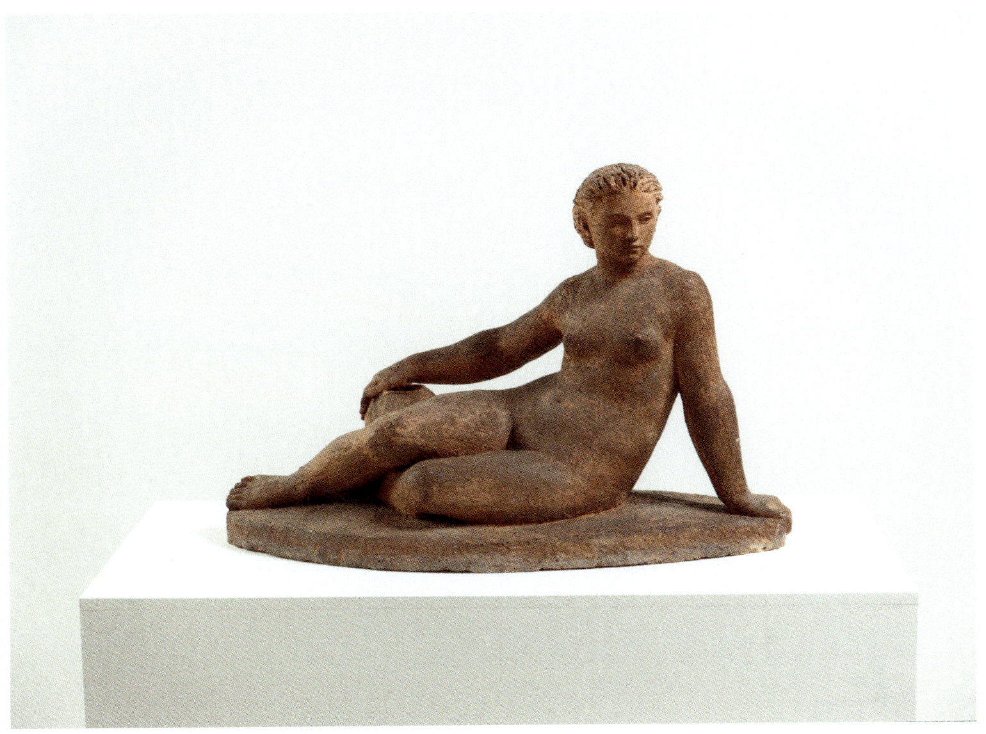

Seated Nude, 1951

KIM
LIM

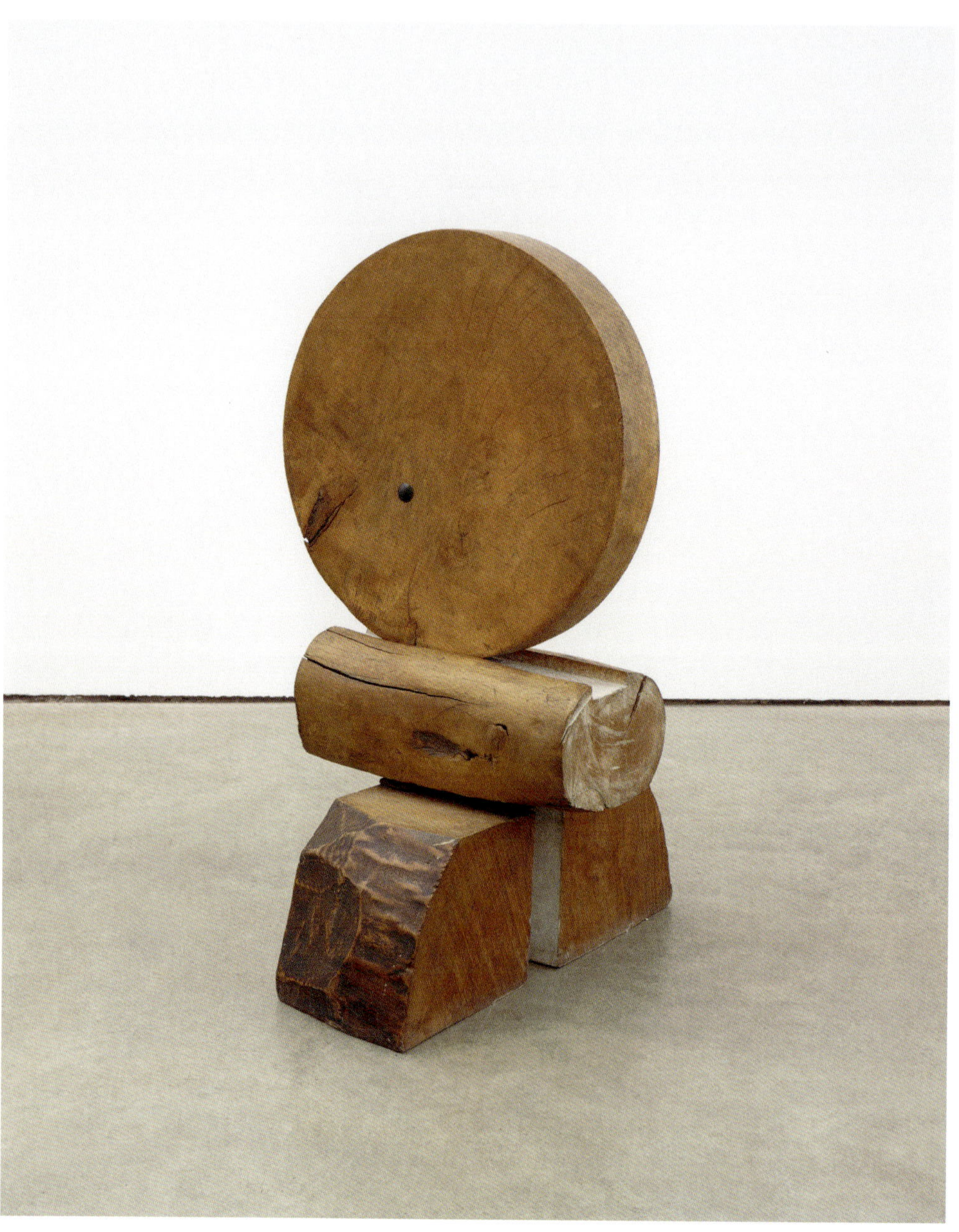

Samurai, 1961

JANN
HAWORTH

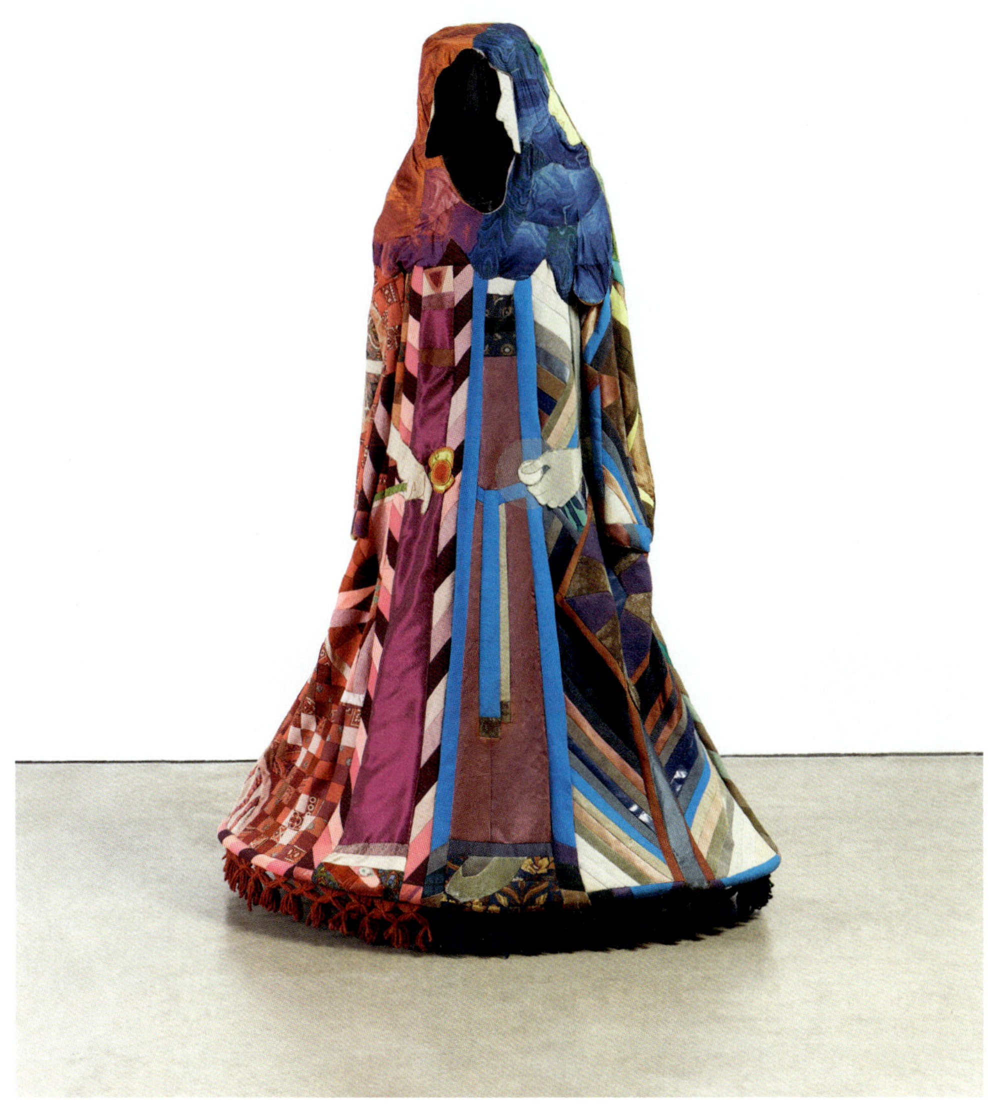

Calendula's Cloak, 1967

JO APPLIN

Jo Applin is Reader in the History of Art at The Courtauld Institute of Art, London, where she teaches modern and contemporary art. A specialist in art since 1960, Applin has written a number of books including: *Lee Lozano: Not Working* (2018); *Alison Wilding*, with Briony Fer (2018)*; London Art Worlds: Mobile, Contingent, and Ephemeral Networks: 1960–1980* (2017); *Eccentric Objects: Rethinking Sculpture in 1960s America* (2012); and *Yayoi Kusama: Infinity Mirror Room – Phalli's Field* (2012). Applin's research addresses questions of abstraction, ageing, eccentricity, feminism, sexuality and subjectivity. She writes book and exhibition reviews for *Artforum* and other publications including *Oxford Art Journal*, *Map*, *Journal of American Studies*, *West 86th*, *Modernism/Modernity*, *The Art Book*, *Sculpture Journal* and the *Times Literary Supplement*.

Firstly, I think it is clear that the contribution of women to the field of modern and contemporary sculpture is immense. But rather than list or generalise, I want to concentrate on two artists whose contribution has been especially significant, not only for my own work, but also the field at large.

Phyllida Barlow and Alison Wilding came out of the British art school system in the 1960s and early 1970s respectively, succeeding in a field then, and arguably still, dominated by men. Both, however, give short shrift to the notion that gender determines the form or meaning of their sculpture, which is not the same as saying that gender doesn't matter. They have each, in their own very different ways, taught me how to think about, look at and teach sculpture. Importantly, neither is much of a polemicist, something I have also always steered clear of. I prefer to take a slower, more circumspect route, and I suspect that this may be one lesson that these two sculptors have taught me.

In 1998, Barlow and Wilding conducted a conversation via fax.[1] The pace of exchange was slower than it would be today due to the technology of that time, resulting in a rewarding, thoughtful back and forth. Among other things (the weather, the sea, a concert on the radio), the two artists discuss the gap between the visual and textual – between what we see and what we say, or are able to say about a sculpture. 'Looking, I think, is a slow burn', wrote Barlow: 'Words are quicker'. Wilding agreed, noting how 'sculpture is that oddball thing that can sidestep language – this is why it frustrates writers'.

Sculpture, for Barlow, 'does not conform to an ordered process of looking akin to "look, then think, then understand: 1+1=2"'. That is too simple, too schematic, and misses the point entirely of what sculpture can do. Instead, Barlow describes sculpture as 'a 1+1=3 experience'. Her point is that the gap between the visual and the textual cannot be bridged; abstract sculpture eludes, it sidesteps; it doesn't answer, it questions. The question is always the thing: in Barlow and Wilding's case, the harder the better. Through the 'slow burn' of the '1+1=3' encounter, sculpture at its best (and Barlow and Wilding are two of the best) thwarts and challenges; it takes its time but it also pulls us up short.

1   'At Sea: A Conversation by Fax Between Phyllida Barlow and Alison Wilding 22.08.98–02.09.98,' reprinted in Mark Godfrey and John Wood, *Phyllida Barlow: Objects For… and Other Things*, (London: Black Dog Publishing), 2004, pp. 81–96

CATHY
DE MONCHAUX

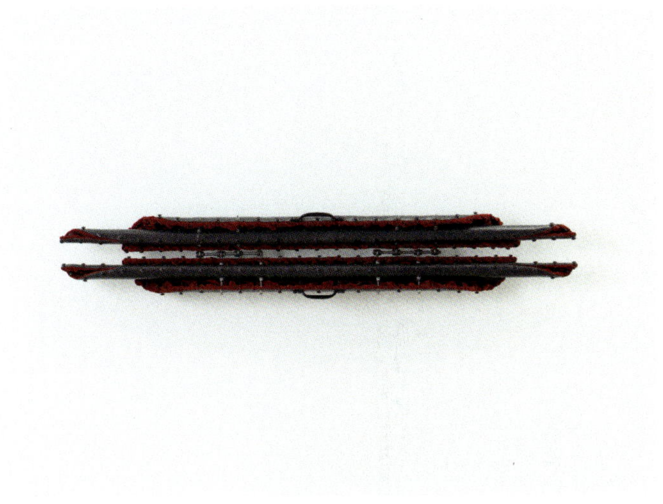

KATHY
PRENDERGAST

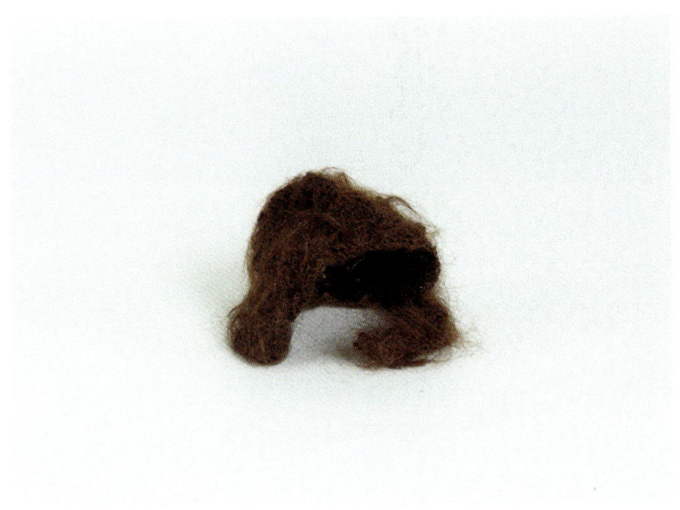

Ferment, 1988 (top); *Hair Bonnet*, 1997 (bottom)

MARY
KELLY

Post-Partum Document, Documentation VI: Pre-Writing Alphabet, Exerque and Diary/Experimentum Mentis VI: (On the Insistence of the Letter), 1978–79

HELEN
CHADWICK

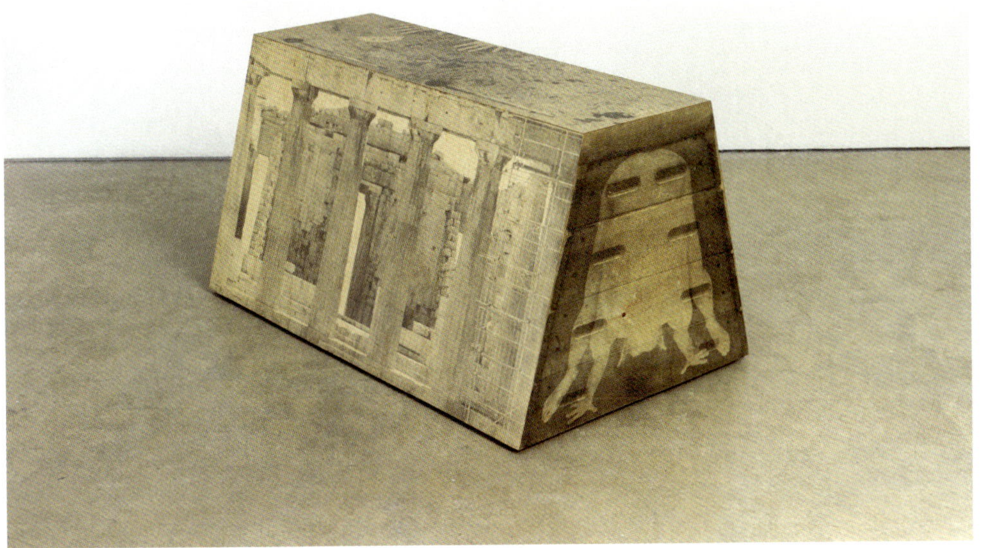

Ego Geometria Sum VIII: The Horse age 11, 1982–83

RANA BEGUM

Rana Begum's work distils spatial and visual experience into ordered form, and through a refined language of minimalist abstraction, Begum blurs the boundaries between sculpture, painting and architecture. Her visual language draws from the urban landscape as well as geometric patterns from traditional Islamic art and architecture. Light is fundamental to her process. Her most recent solo exhibitions include: *Perception and Reflection*, Third Line Gallery, Dubai, 2019; Christian Lethert, Cologne, 2018; *Space Light Color*, Djanogly Art Gallery, University of Nottingham, 2018; and *Conversation with Light and Colour*, Gallery 10, Tate St Ives, 2018. Begum received the Jack Goldhill Award for Sculpture in 2012 and the Abraaj Group Art Prize in 2017.

Throughout my life, from growing up in Bangladesh to living here in the UK, I have found that issues of gender and race are ever present, sometimes feeling like a determining factor in what I can do or how far I can go. I have had to push very hard in order for my work to stand alone and not be viewed through the lenses of gender, race or religion.

I have worked alongside a number of inspiring women, both curators and artists, who have helped me to expand my practice and navigate the art world in all its complexity. Following graduation, I assisted artist Tess Jaray for a number of years, an experience through which I gained the confidence to truly explore and embrace colour as a medium in its own right.

My breakthrough came when I showed at Dhaka Art Summit in 2014, which was followed by a solo show at Parasol Unit in 2016. When I was first approached by curator Diana Betancourt about doing a project in Dhaka, I had many conflicting emotions. I was nervous about what it meant to show my work in Bangladesh – a place I felt at once connected to, yet very distant from. While creating this work I felt like I was also making an emotional journey, contemplating many things – my roots, my childhood and my contrasting present.

The show at Parasol Unit felt more like

a consolidation of my artistic career to date and illustrated to me how my research has evolved and how certain elements have come in and out of focus over the years.

Above all, these breakthrough shows made me realise what a difference it can make to both your practice and your career when people demonstrate belief in what you are doing. These kinds of opportunities are instrumental in creating a dialogue with other curators and institutions, which in turn challenges your work and ensures it continues to grow and evolve.

HOLLY
HENDRY

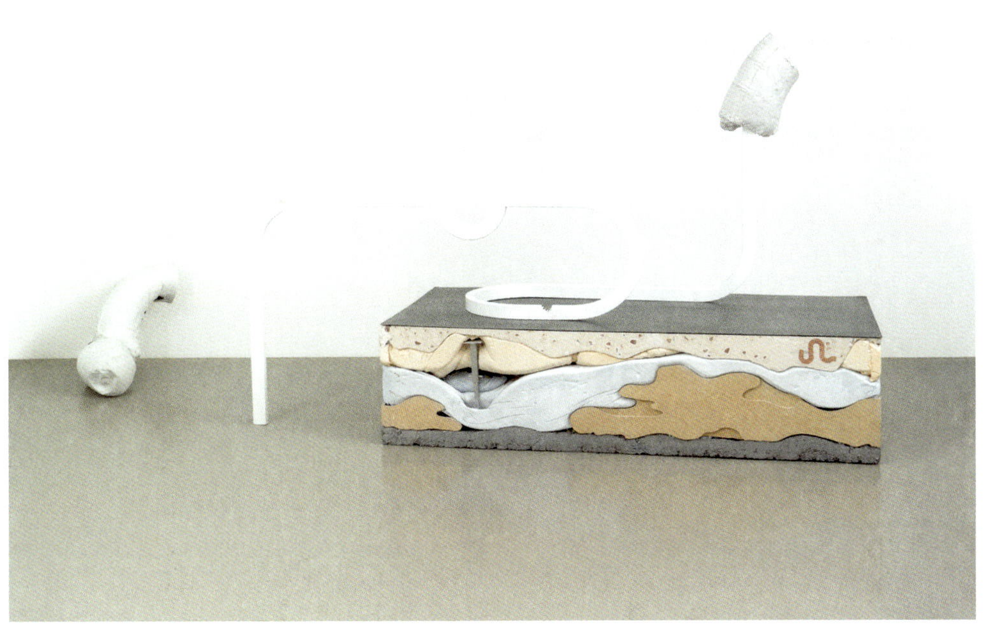

Gut Feelings (Stromatolith), 2016

REBECCA
WARREN

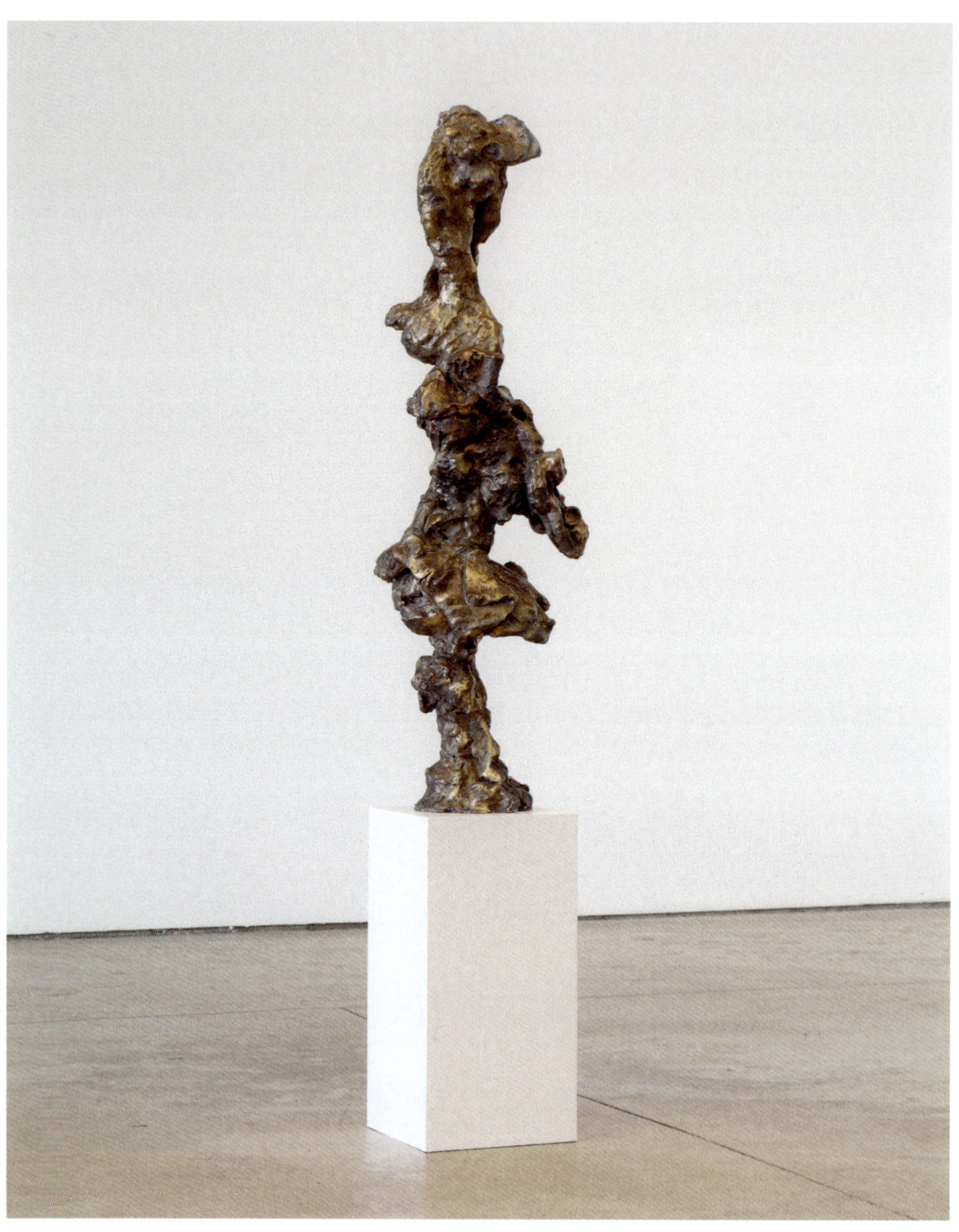

Regine, 2007

SARAH
LUCAS

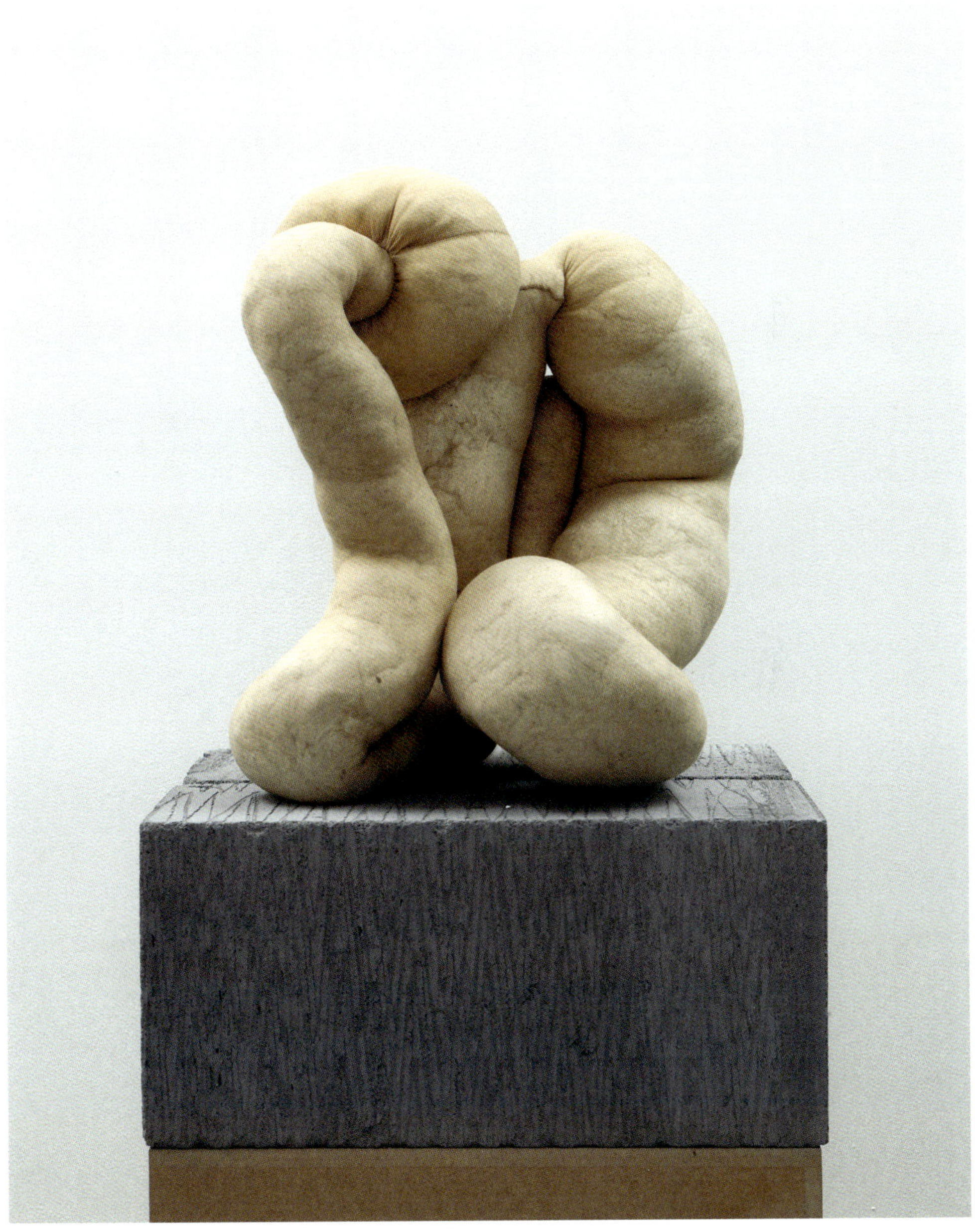

NUD CYCLADIC 7, 2010

ALICE CHANNER

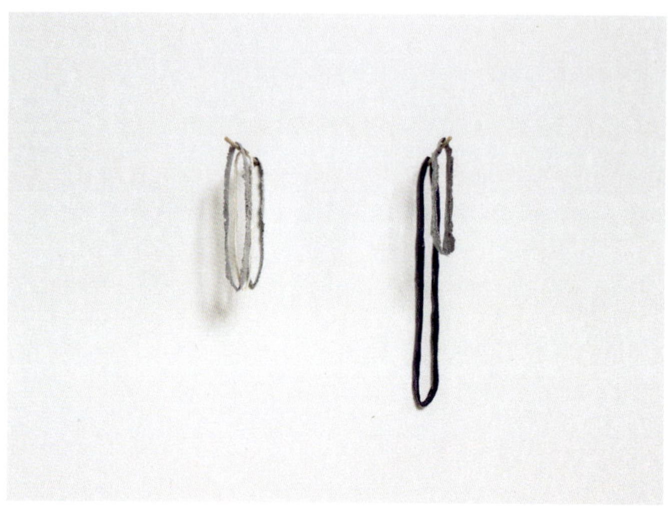

JANE COYLE

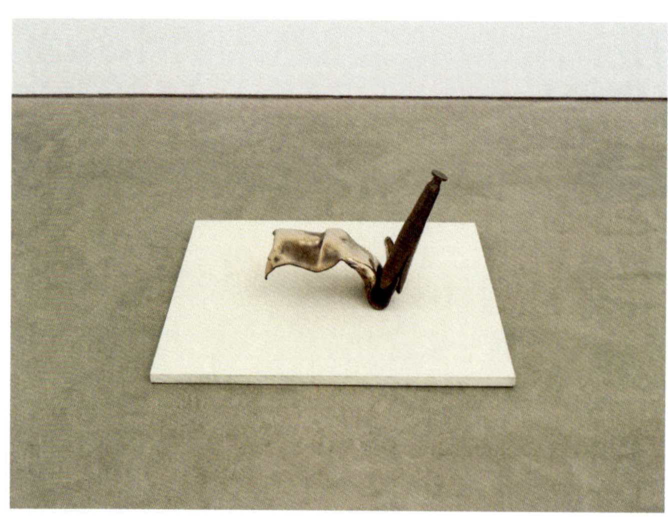

Maxi, Mini, Midi, Midi, Midi (Mauve and Cream), 2012 (top); *Peg*, 1966 (bottom)

AMALIA PICA

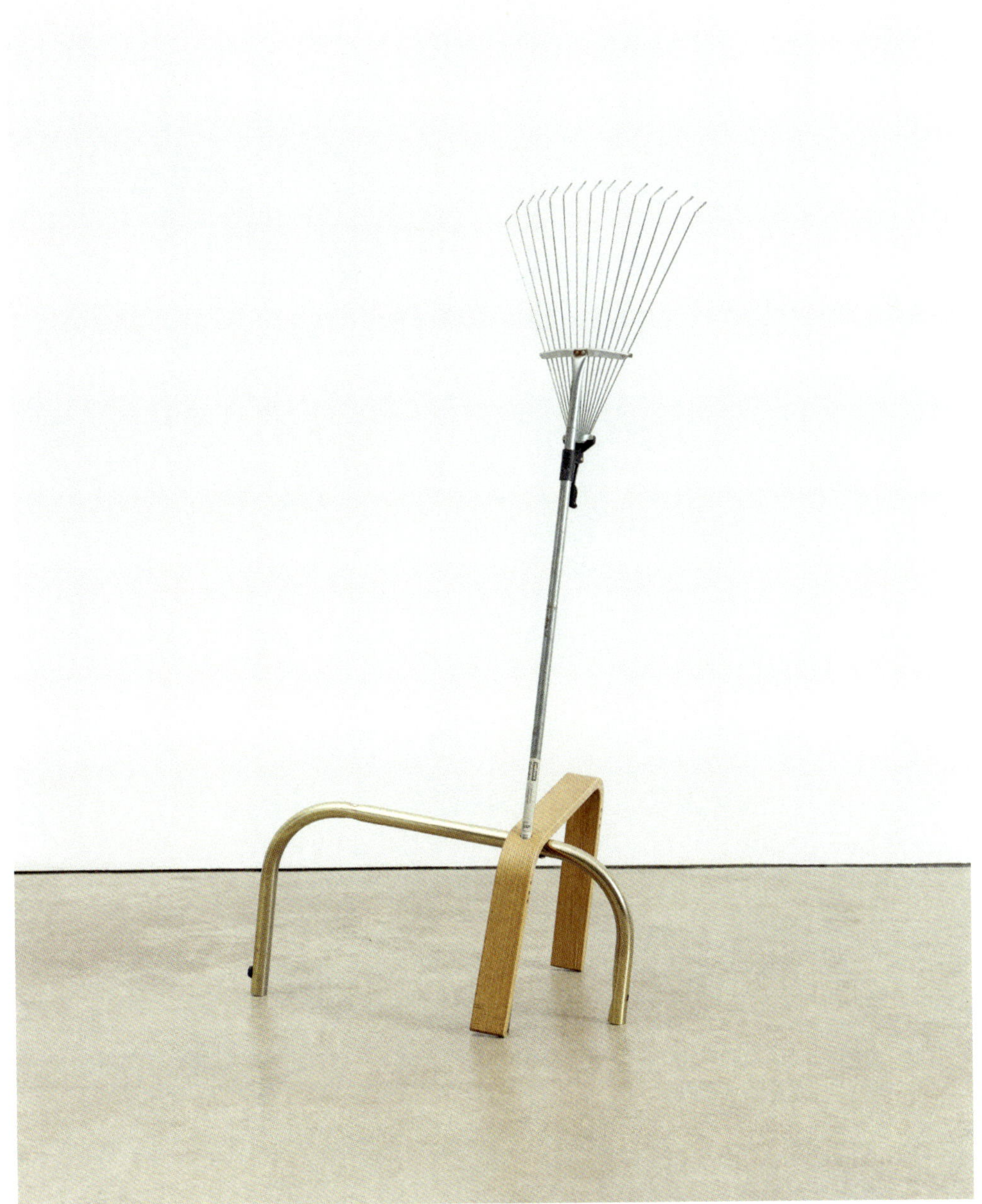

Catachresis #40 (teeth of the rake, leg of the chair, leg of the table, head of the screw), 2013

PENELOPE CURTIS

Penelope Curtis has been Director of the Gulbenkian Museum in Lisbon since 2015. Her curatorial career began at Tate Liverpool, after which she led the Henry Moore Institute, Leeds, before moving on to become Director of Tate Britain in 2010. Known best as an expert on modern and contemporary sculpture, her books include *Vertical, Horizontal, Open, Closed: Sculpture* (2017), *Patio and Pavilion: The Place of Sculpture in Modern Architecture* (2007/08) and *Sculpture 1900–45: After Rodin* (1999). During her career, Curtis has been steadily more able to include a higher number of women in collection displays, acquisitions and exhibition programmes.

It is ironic, perhaps, that this survey begins
with Barbara Hepworth, who hated to be
described in terms of her gender. Though
we may be accustomed to the reasons for
positive discrimination, surely now we need
to go beyond them. This would mean making
a more fully historical analysis – which would
need, perforce, to include male artists – and
to present it in terms of statistics. We may
be tired of data collection, but in this field
it is patently lacking. What was the position
of the female artist in the second half of the
twentieth century? How common or rare was
she in relation to her peers at art school, her
fellow teachers? In the purchases made for
our national collections, on the purchasing
committees of those collections, and so forth?
What is the graphic that would describe her
typical trajectory? And how does it relate to
the gender of the curator?

And here we are looking not so much
at the female artist, but at the female sculptor,
who needs, perhaps, to be distinguished from
those who became designers, ceramicists,
jewellers, etc. In contrast to women architects,
whose role has emerged often in collaboration
(think Lilly Reich, Alison Smithson, Franca Helg,
for example), women sculptors have generally
been single figures, whose very activity as
volumetric thinkers caused consternation.

The woman sculptor had already emerged

in modern Britain, historically speaking, with Anne Seymour Damer, and then with Mary Thornycroft, Lady Feodora Gleichen and Princess Louise, Duchess of Argyll, and tended, like other types of artist, to be associated with high birth and means. This is in marked contrast to the male sculptors of the turn of the century – Auguste Rodin, Antoine Bourdelle or Constantin Brâncuși – who deliberately played on their plebeian roots. This same paradigm was to be played out between Henry Moore and Hepworth, the 'working class' versus the 'bourgeoise', the 'authentic' versus the 'refined'.

How many of these artists were married to fellow artists? Barbara Hepworth, Rosemary Young, Kim Lim, Mary Martin, Rachel Whiteread, to name a few. How would Young's career have been different if she had not lived with Reg Butler and devoted herself to a joint project that went under his name?

What is special about sculpture by women, in comparison to sculpture by men? And what is special about sculpture by women, in comparison to painting by women? Are we looking at something that can be described on its own terms? I think it is dangerous to do this, but perhaps, nonetheless, one might consider the way in which women sculptors helped to take sculpture off the plinth, to reduce it in scale, to make it in new materials, forms and colours. We could, I think, trace some lines here which include the embracing of 'soft' materials and patterning, which have long been associated with the 'minor' arts, but which have at last come to be seen as important as any other means. How many male sculptors do we now understand to have identified and borrowed from these vocabularies? I could name several, but that is (perhaps) another story.

LILIANE LIJN

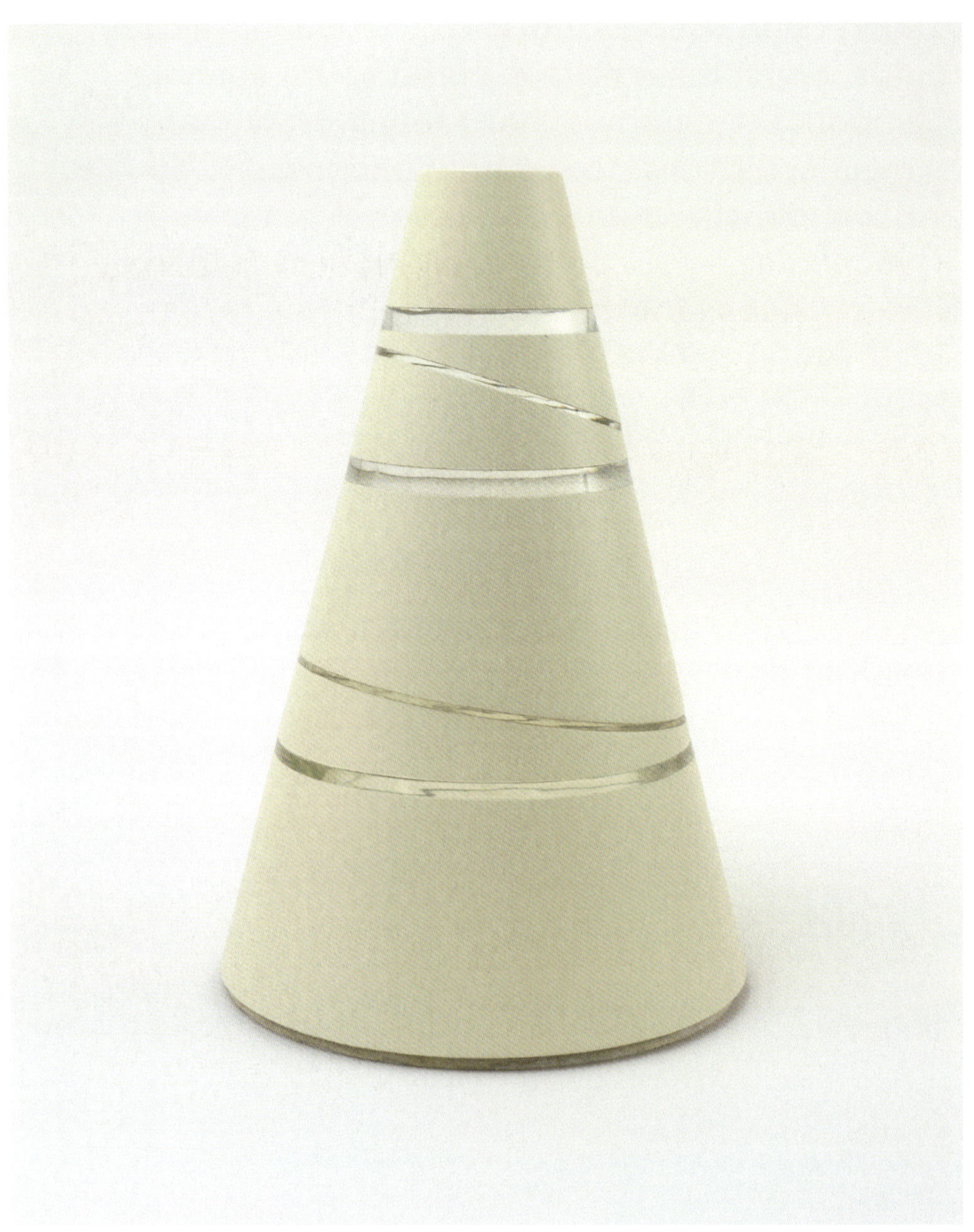

See Thru Koan, 1969

MONA HATOUM

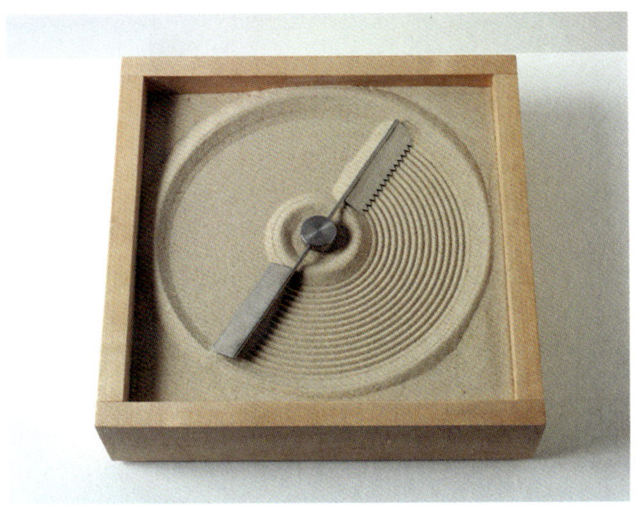

MARY MARTIN

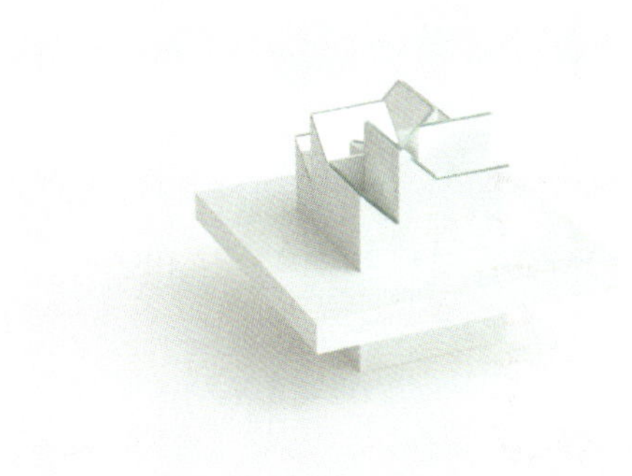

+ and -, 1994 (top); *Rotation*, 1966 (bottom)

JESSIE FLOOD-PADDOCK

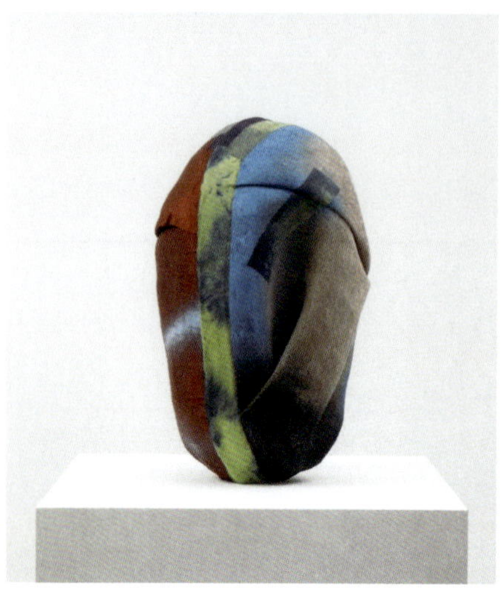

SUSAN COLLIS

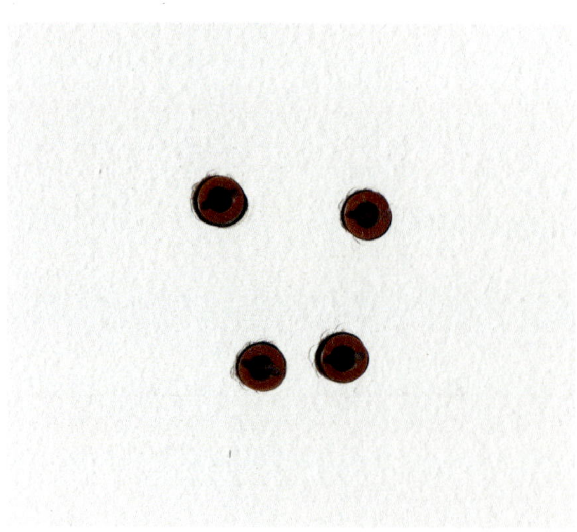

Snack 16, 2015 (top); *Untitled (rawl plugs)*, 2007 (bottom)

PHYLLIDA
BARLOW

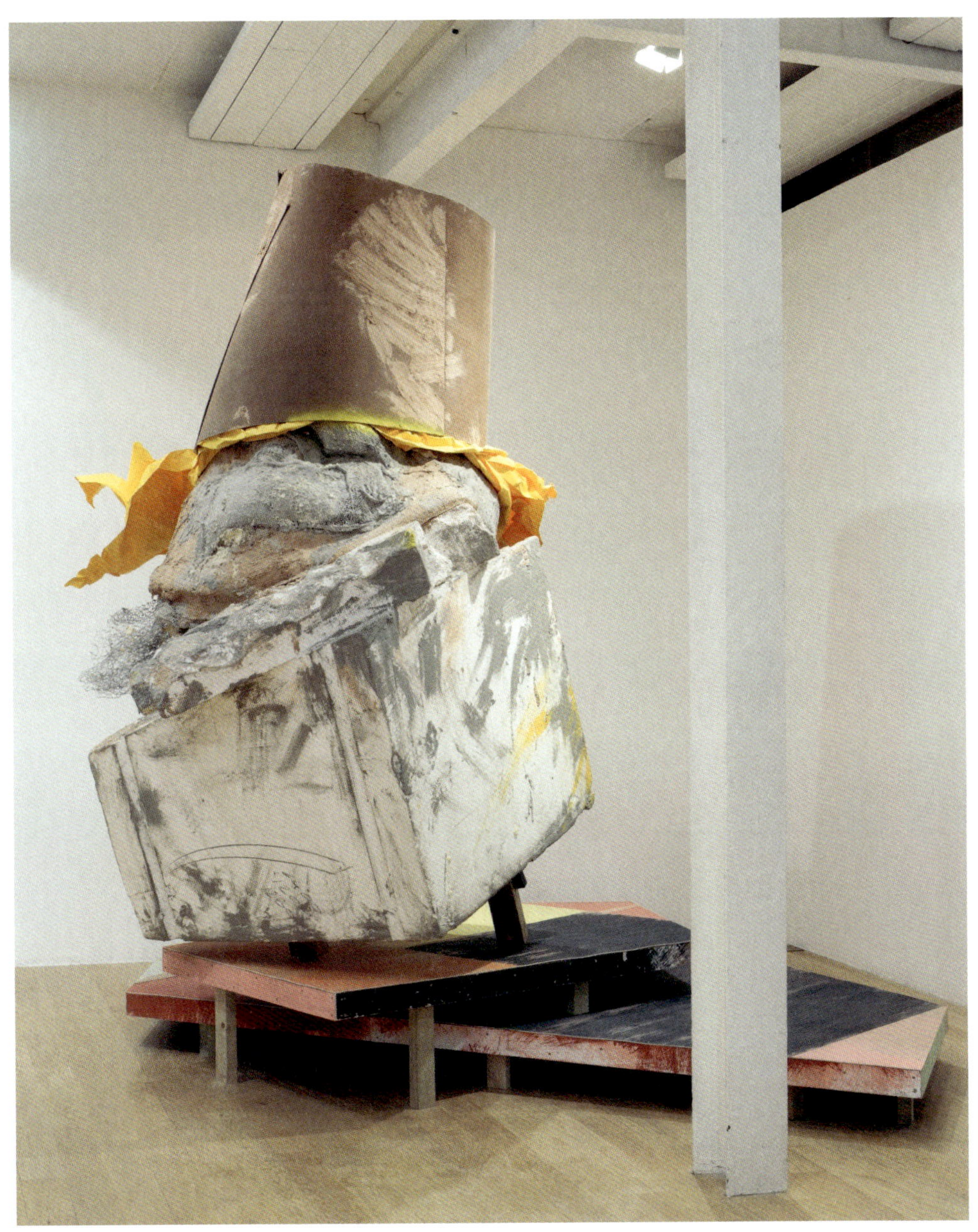

untitled: dunce, 2015

HILARY GRESTY

Hilary Gresty has an MPhil from The Courtauld Institute of Art, London, and has worked in the visual arts for over four decades. She is a freelance writer, researcher and lecturer. Gresty was director of Kettle's Yard during the 1980s and went on to establish a professional association for gallery directors and curators, VAGA (Visual Arts and Galleries Association). She began researching the lives and careers of women sculptors whilst working at Lincoln University between 2012 and 2016. Working with Catherine George (Coventry University), Gresty established the ongoing research project, *Women Working in Sculpture from 1960 to the Present Day: Towards a New Lexicon*, in 2016.

My interest in sculpture began when I started exploring the origins of early 1970s conceptual and non-object based work. In the UK this work had strong, but not exclusive links to the male-dominated St Martin's School of Art sculpture department. Likewise, time-based work provided a neutral, flexible and affordable space for many women.

In the mid 1980s I worked with Cornelia Parker, Mona Hatoum, Phyllida Barlow and Veronica Ryan as well as Mary Kelly and Susan Hiller, all of whom were inspirational in pushing the boundaries of art forms, conventions and subject matter. Despite the achievements of these and others such as Wendy Taylor and Liliane Lijn, a catalogue trawl reveals a stark disparity between the profiles of men and women featured, and exposes the fragility of the history beyond that which is published. To take one example: the catalogue for *Modern British Sculpture* (Royal Academy, 2011). This exhibition included 50 men, 11 women and one family group. A work by Tony Cragg adorns the catalogue cover, whilst one by Rose Finn-Kelcey was chosen for the more ephemeral gallery guide.

The higher ratio of women versus men completing fine art courses compared with the number who go on to have a career rooted in art only emphasises this embedded inequality. The Royal College of Art (RCA) only appointed its first female fine art professor, Jo Stockham, in 2008 and the Royal Academy, the first female professor of sculpture, Cathie Pilkington, in 2015. These significant appointments are reported to have induced greater collaboration, a kinder overall ethic and to have enhanced the confidence of women.

In interviewing a number of women for the research project *Women Working in Sculpture from 1960 to the Present Day: Towards a New Lexicon*, we have found that the social and cultural factors that affect women's careers appear remarkably intransigent. Women often have fragmented working lives or modify their practice for family reasons. As one said, babies and stone carving dust do not mix. Another, frequently flying across the Atlantic to see her family, now makes suitcase-sized work, adapting as necessary to her situation.

An increase in the number of international students has further diversified cultural expectations, and the window onto misogyny opened up by social media has reframed feminism. However, meeting with recent RCA graduates as part of this project revealed the striking persistence of outmoded attitudes, such as the unwillingness of male students to engage with work that touches on female subjectivity. Tutors and students alike have called for a revised attitude to a woman's age and a recasting of traditional career paths.

GILLIAN LOWNDES

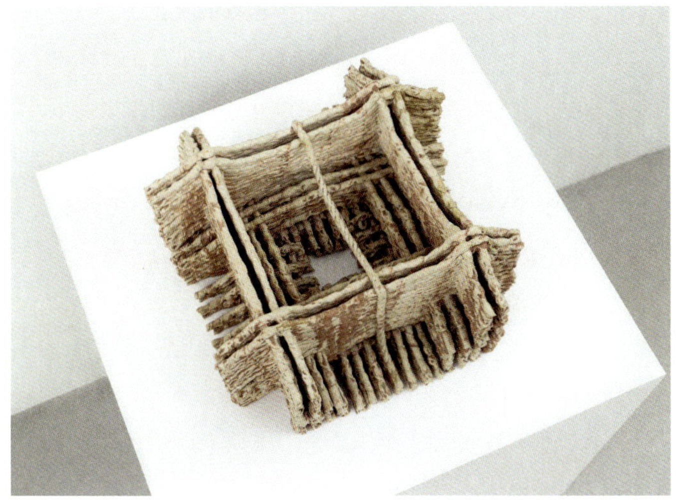

ANTHEA ALLEY

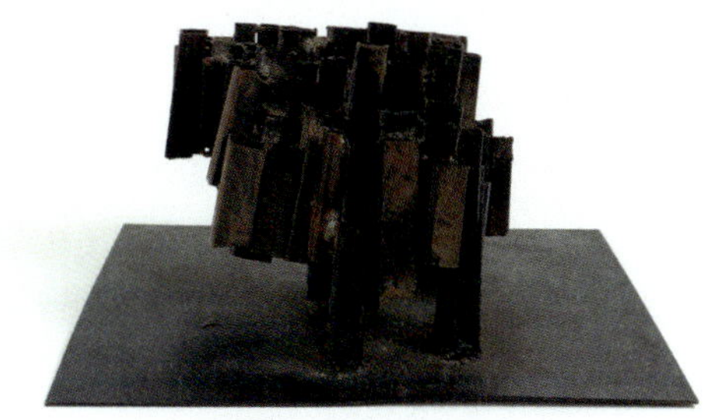

Untitled, 1976 (top); *Rock*, 1964 (bottom)

BARBARA
HEPWORTH

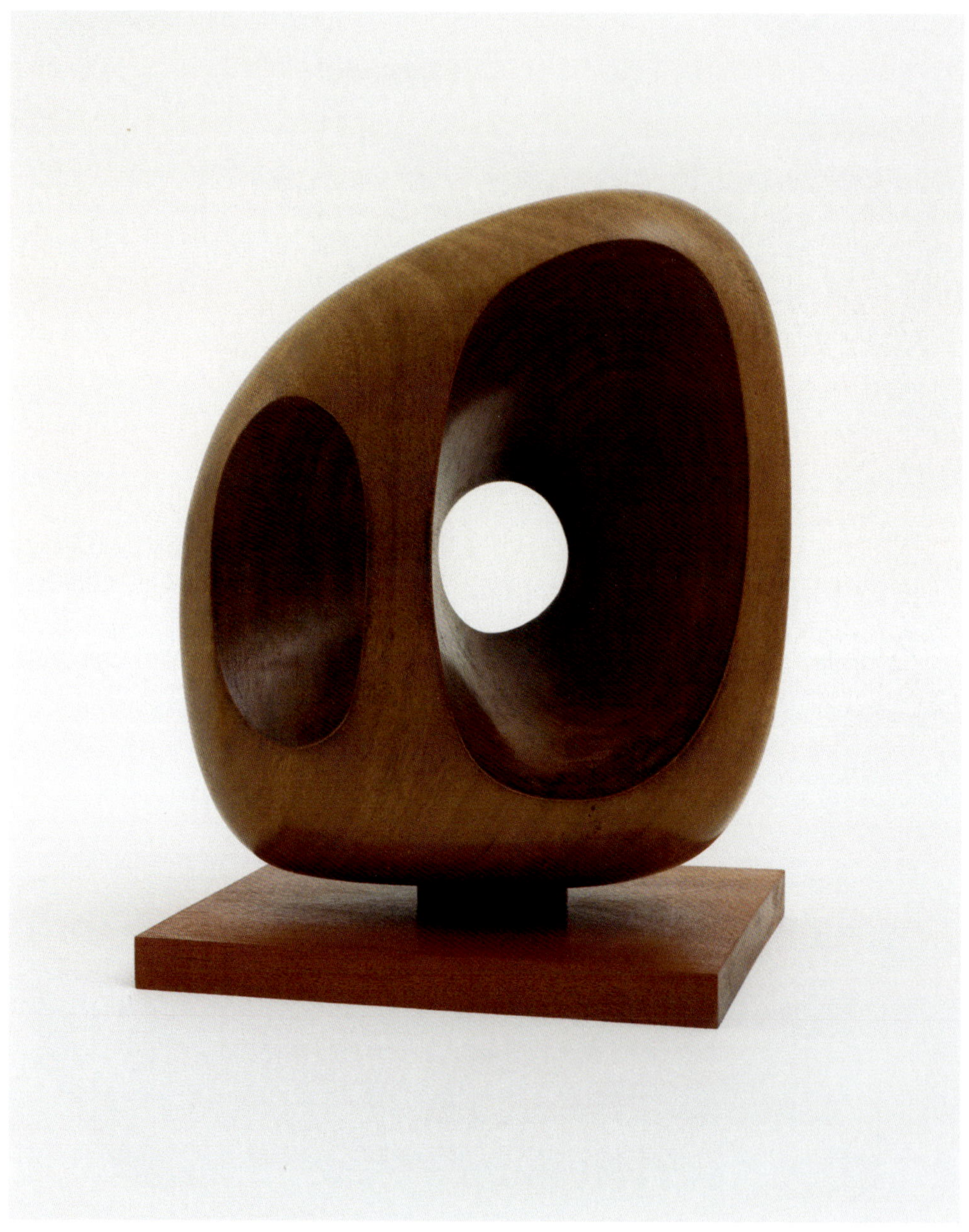

Icon, 1957

VERONICA
RYAN

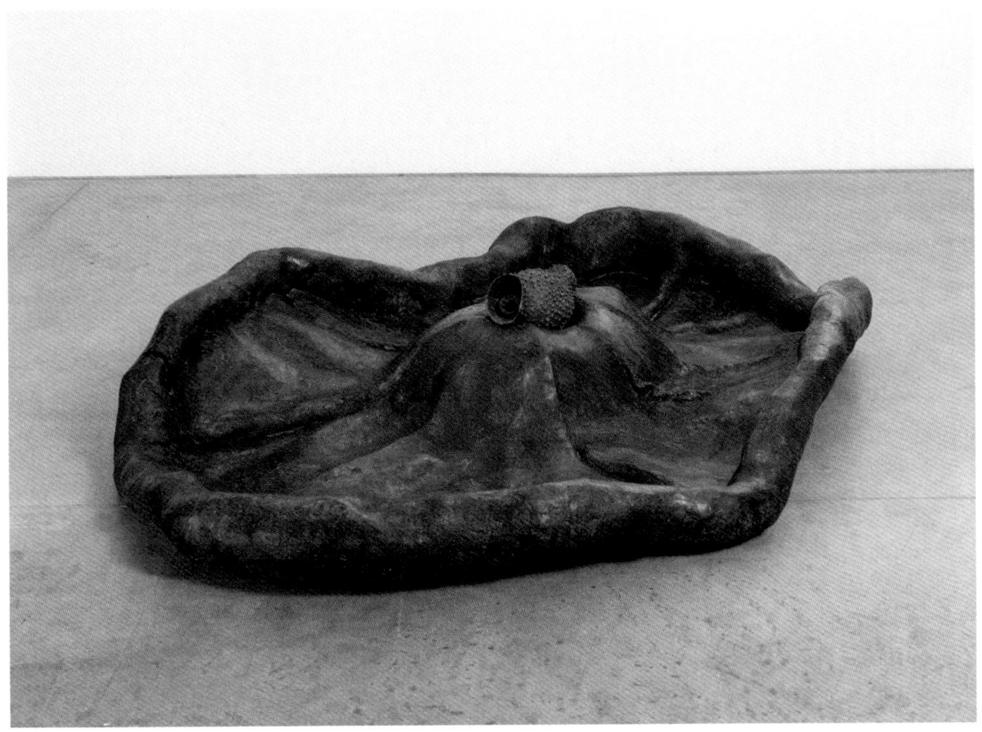

Territorial, 1986

SHIRAZEH HOUSHIARY

Shirazeh Houshiary was born in Iran in 1955 and went on to study at Chelsea School of Art (1976–79). She quickly became established at the forefront of the younger generation of sculptors working in Britain in the 1980s, and her work was included in important group exhibitions such as *Aperto '82*, XL Venice Biennale in 1982, and *Les Magiciens de la Terre* at the Centre Georges Pompidou, Paris in 1989.

Houshiary's first solo show at Lisson Gallery, London was in 1984, and she has gone on to show at many major galleries both as a solo artist and in group shows. She was shortlisted for the Turner Prize at the Tate Gallery in 1994, and was awarded the title Professor at the London Institute in 1997. Houshiary lives and works in London.

My early sculptures were made of clay and straw, and their surfaces gradually became covered with grey-green mould. They were fragile and mysterious.

In 1982, I exhibited five of these sculptures at the Serpentine Gallery under the collective title *Listen to the Tale of the Reed*. The Arts Council acquired one of the pieces for their collection and this was the first time I had sold a sculpture. Their support and interest in these works started my journey.

At the time, there were few women artists, especially sculptors, and the art world was male dominated. There was a palpable sense of hostility towards female artists. I was young and I had to find a way to break through.

I struggled with many colleagues who believed that women could not be great artists and with museum directors who believed, therefore, that that is the reason women have no history in the arts.

Sarah Kent wrote in a *Time Out* review of young British sculptors in November 1982: 'I would like to see more of Iranian artist Shirazeh Houshiary's interesting sculptures. There is a combination of rural intelligence and urban sophistication in this dark and compelling presence.' I began to participate in many exhibitions under the umbrella of the 'Young British Sculptors'. I needed to be different. These early works seem to me to speak of a quest for reconnecting to the earth and its imagination. Perhaps my voice is more relevant now, with a growing awareness of an impending environmental crisis, the lack of respect for our planet and the growth of nationalism.

Since the early 1990s I have become increasingly aware of, and at odds with, the many voices promoting nationality-driven exhibitions. This idea has dominated the stage for more than two decades, bringing much division in the world.

These prejudices have shaped the way women artists have been seen through time. It is not just about success or failure in the art world but how women's art has been framed. Can we ever be free from all the clichés regarding who we are? It is truly sad that many mediocre male artists are still being celebrated in museums and art institutions whilst many intelligent and sensitive women have been ignored or even wrongly portrayed.

HAYLEY TOMPKINS

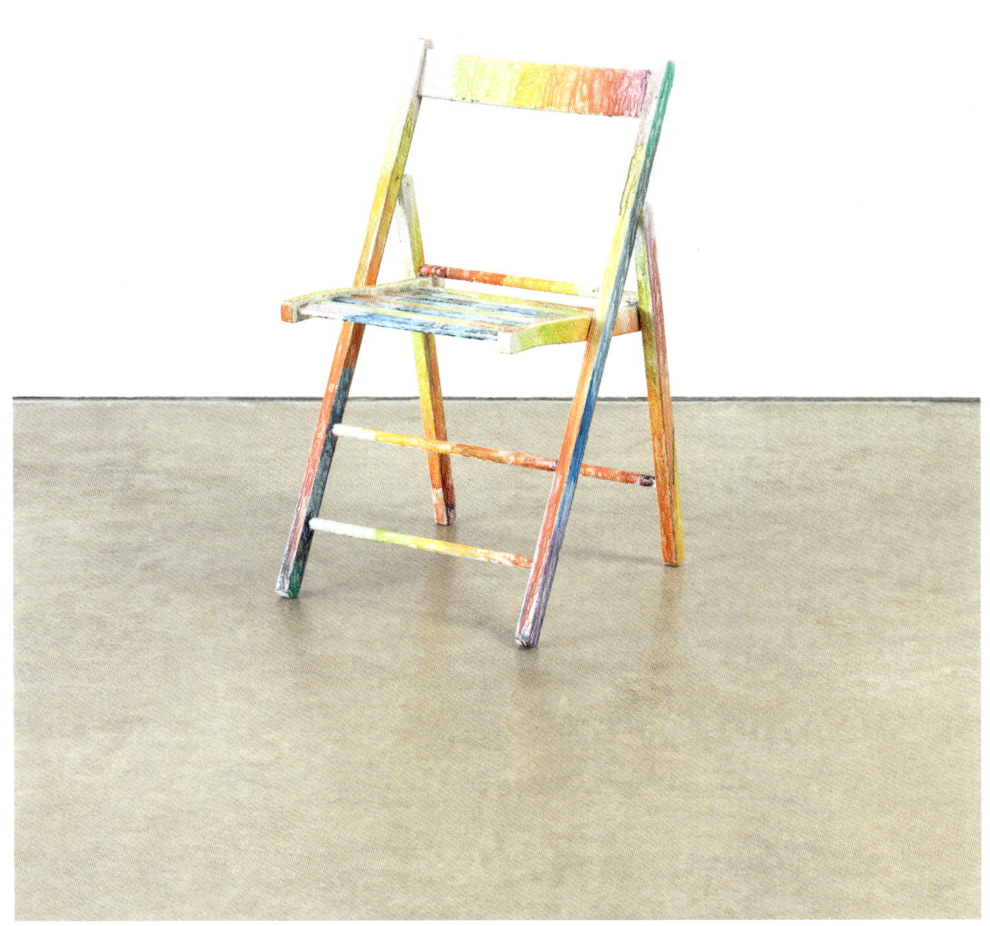

Chair, 2011

HELEN
MARTEN

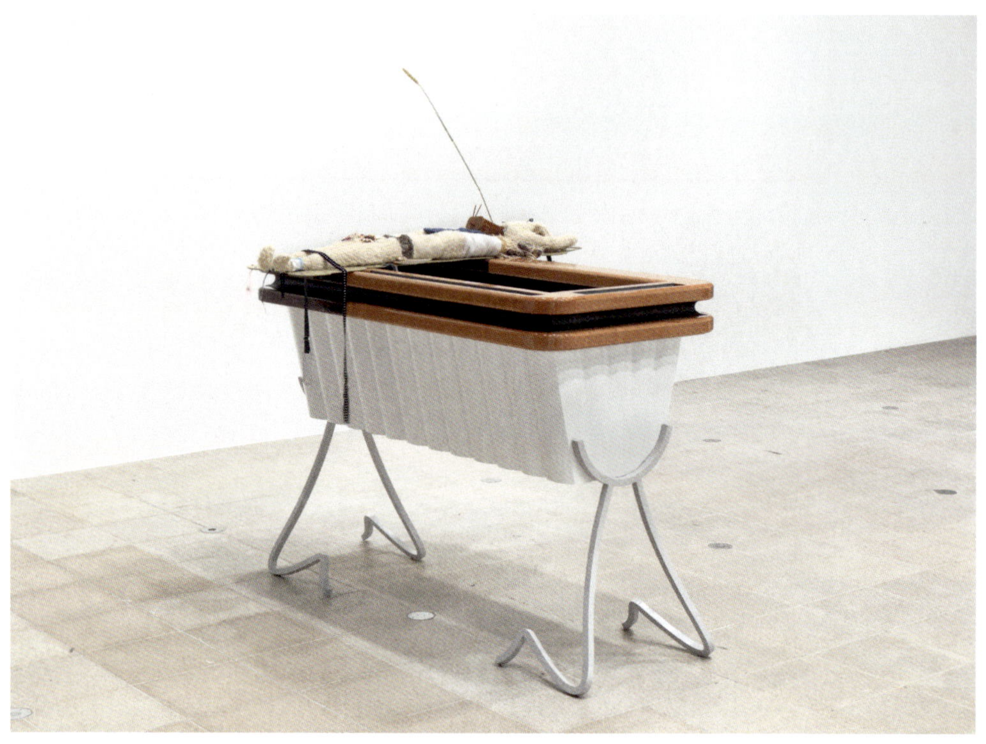

Bluebutter Idles, 2014

ANYA
GALLACCIO

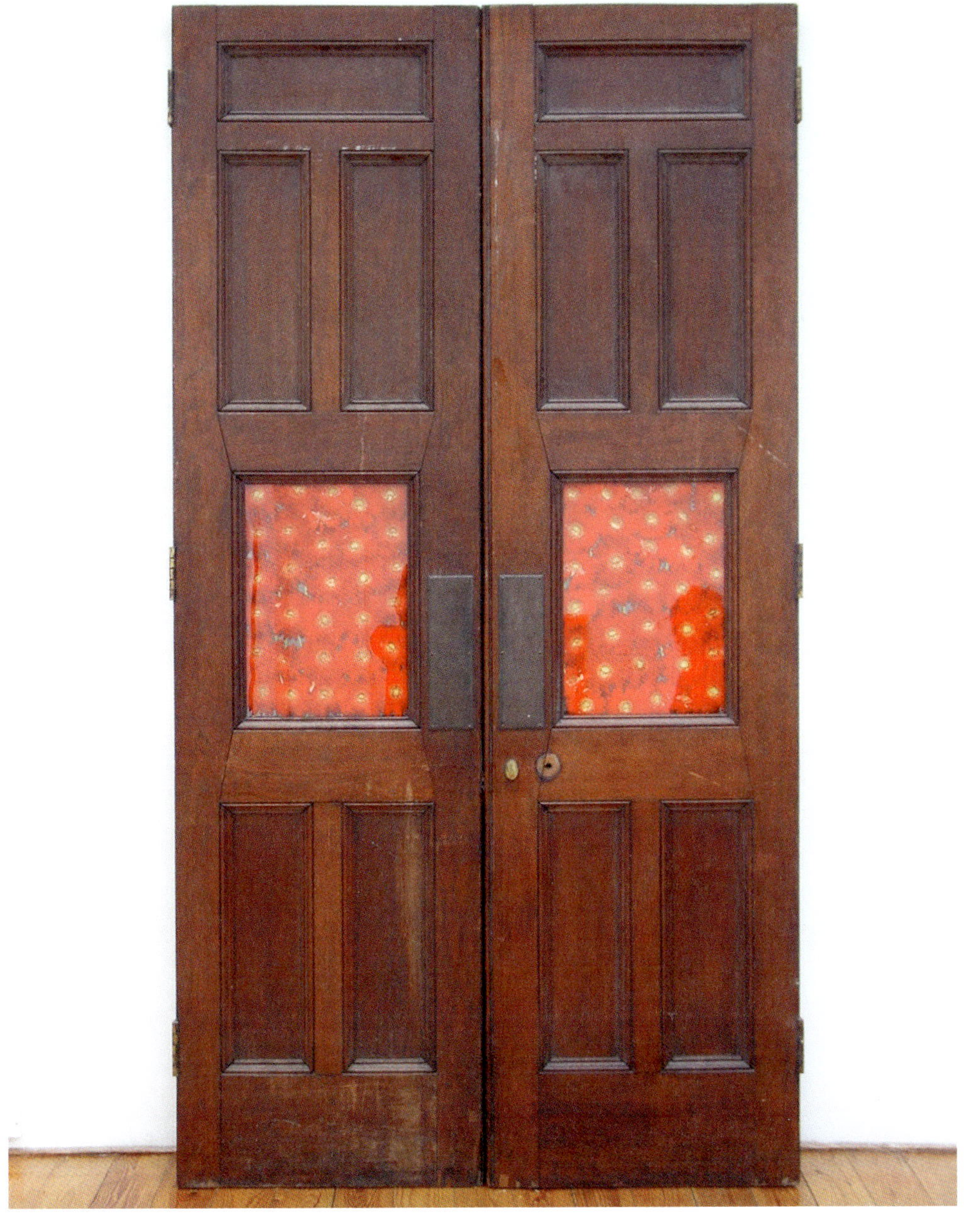

can love remember the question and the answer, 2003

SARAH KENT

Sarah Kent began contributing to art magazines such as *Studio International*, *Flash Art*, *Art in America* and *Modern Painters* in 1971. She was Visual Arts Editor of *Time Out, London* for 30 years and continues to write regularly for *The Arts Desk*. Having studied painting at the Slade, she was a practising artist and lecturer until 1977 when she became Director of Exhibitions at the ICA. She has sat on numerous juries including the Turner Prize, Schweppes Photographic Portrait Prize and New Contemporaries. Her books include *Shelagh Wakely: Thinking Aloud* and *Michelle Stuart: The Nature of Time* (2019); *Composition* (1995); *Shark-Infested Waters* (1994); *Elisabeth Frink: Sculpture and Drawings 1952–1984* (1985); *Women's Images of Men* with Jacqueline Morreau (1985); *Berlin: a Critical View, Ugly Realism 20s–70s* with Eckhart Gillen (1978).

Most of the sculptures I love are by women;
here are a few.

Including a coil of wire pinioned by a
brick and a spiral of wire nailed to the floor,
Shelagh Wakely's *Some Encounters with Reality*
(1977) seemed like energy held in check. Some
20 years later, she imprisoned cherries, plums
and courgettes within delicate wire cages
and left them to rot while others, sheathed
in gold leaf, were left to wither into exquisite
memento mori.

In the early 1990s, Anya Gallaccio also
espoused the beauty of decay by leaving a
ton of oranges to moulder on a warehouse
floor (*Tense*, 1990), sandwiching 800 gerberas
against the window of Karsten Schubert's
gallery (*preserve 'beauty'*, 1991) and carpeting
the ICA with 10,000 dying roses (*Red on
Green*, 1992). Cornelia Parker blew up a shed
and hung the remnants from the ceiling, like
exploding shrapnel (*Cold Dark Matter*, 1991)
and in a futile bid to conserve memories,
Rachel Whiteread mummified a room in
plaster (*Ghost*, 1990).

Phyllida Barlow pioneered the slacker
aesthetic. Made from studio clutter, her ad
hoc installations are glorious monuments
to anti-heroism; meanwhile Sarah Lucas
explores the erotic potential of mundane
objects. *Au Natural* (1994) invokes a sex romp
between a bucket and two melons, on one

hand, and two oranges and a cucumber, on the other.

Why am I drawn to these remarkable sculptors? Because, in their work, loss and destruction are catalysts for creativity. They embrace fragility, transience, degradation and decay – contingencies that sculpture traditionally has sought to overcome – with a lightness of touch that gainsays any hint of pomposity or self-aggrandisement.

GRACE SCHWINDT

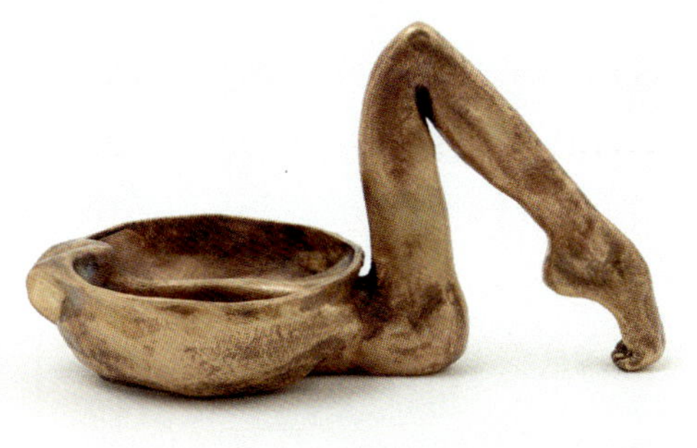

KATIE CUDDON

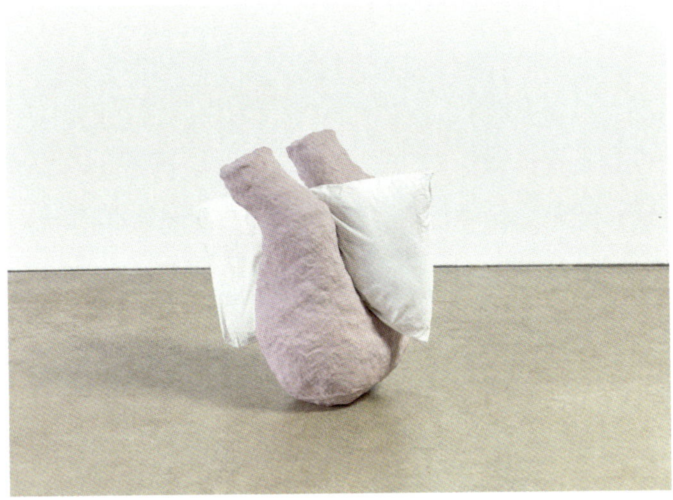

Position, 2018 (top); *A Problem of Departure*, 2013 (bottom)

ROSEMARY
YOUNG

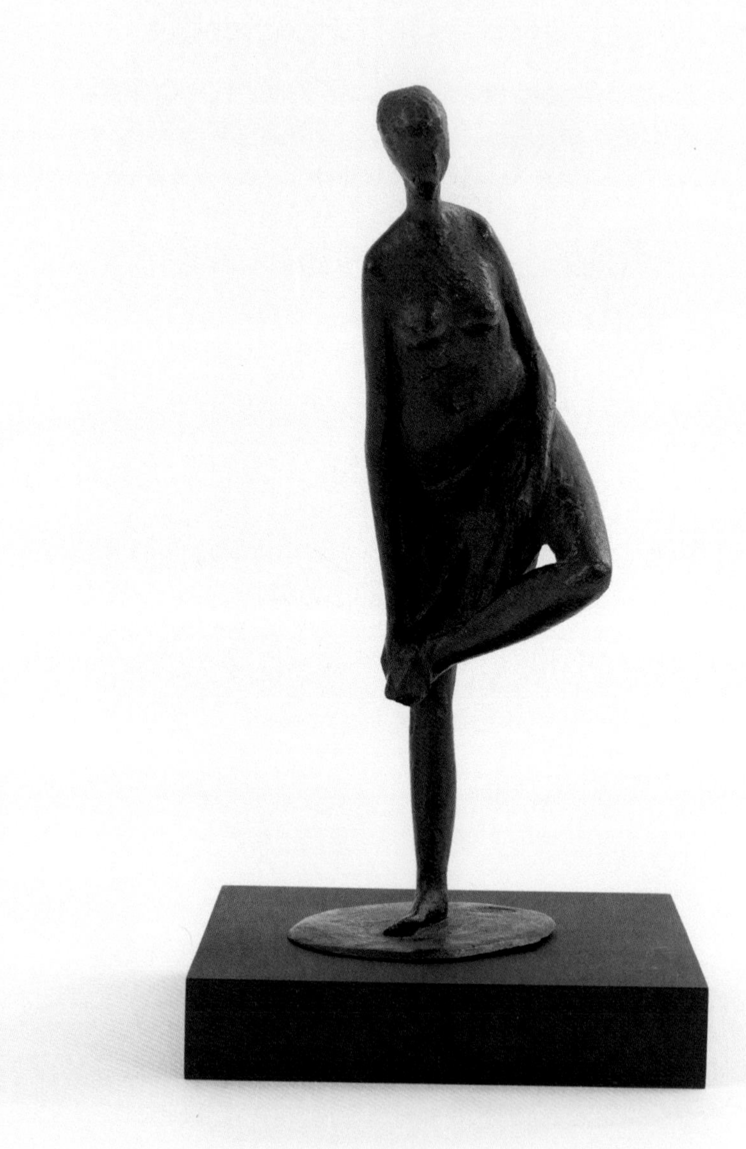

Girl Drying Her Foot, undated

ANTHEA HAMILTON

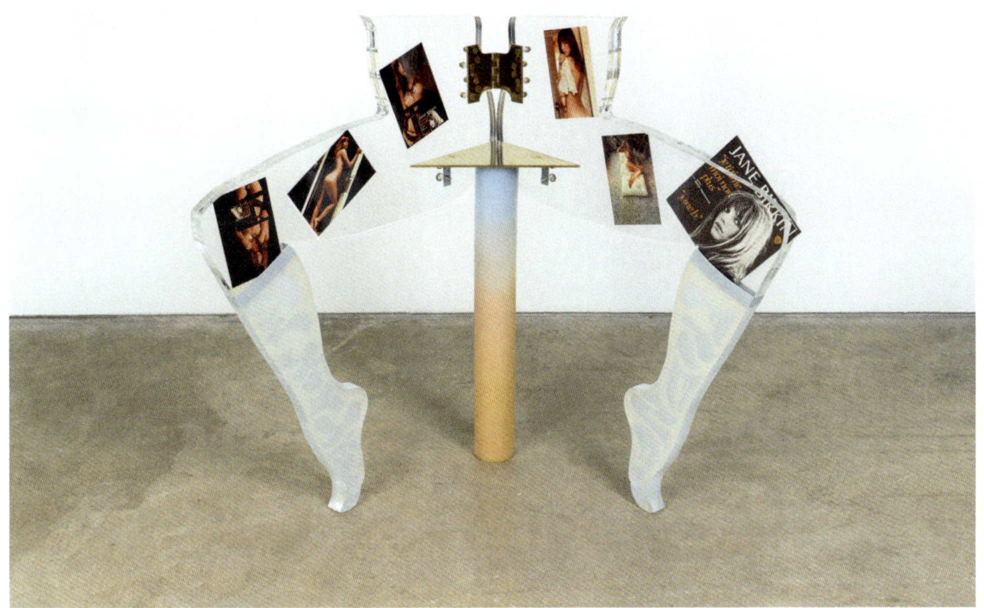

Leg Chair (Jane Birkin), 2011

RANA
BEGUM

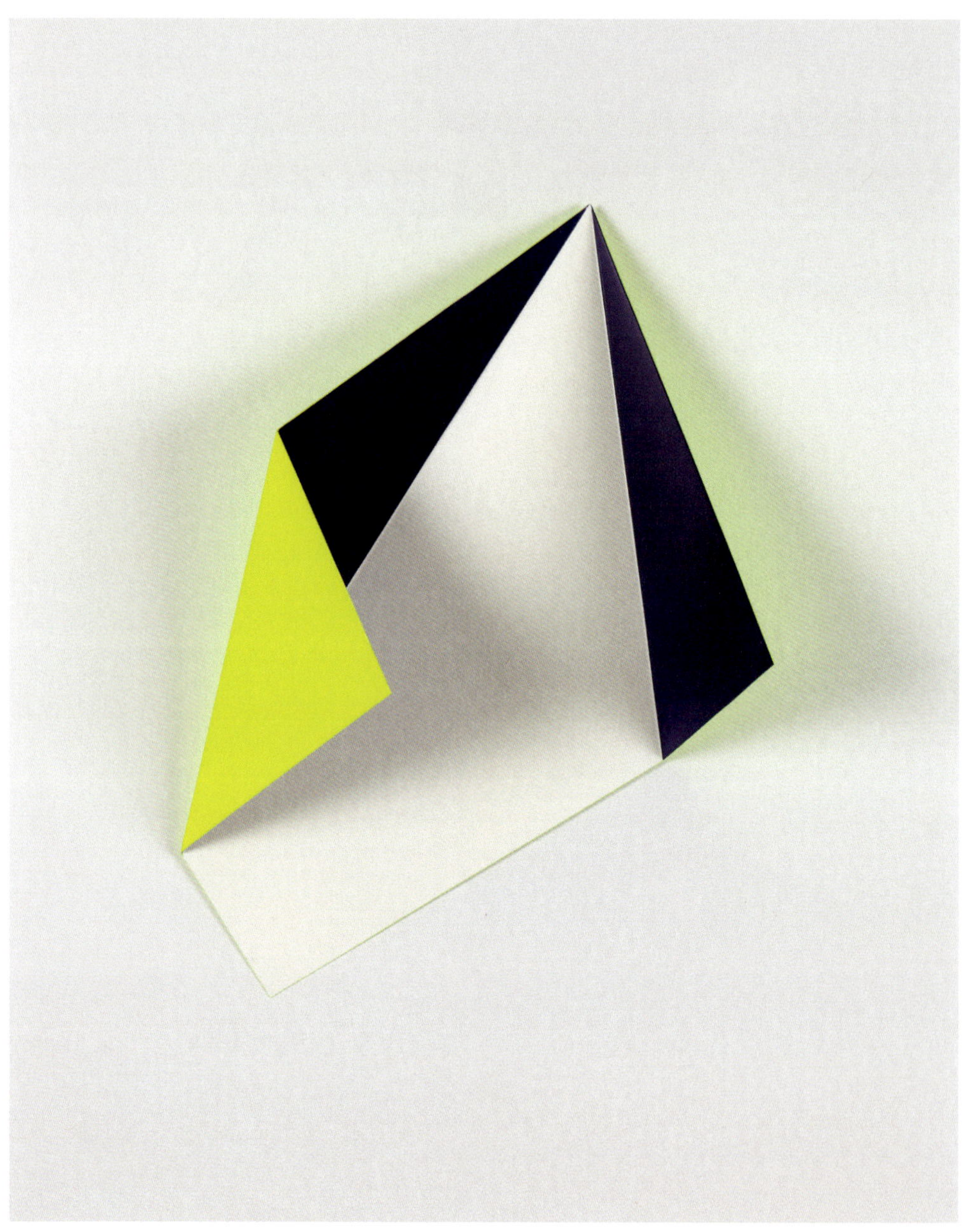

No. 429 SFold, 2013

EVA ROTHSCHILD

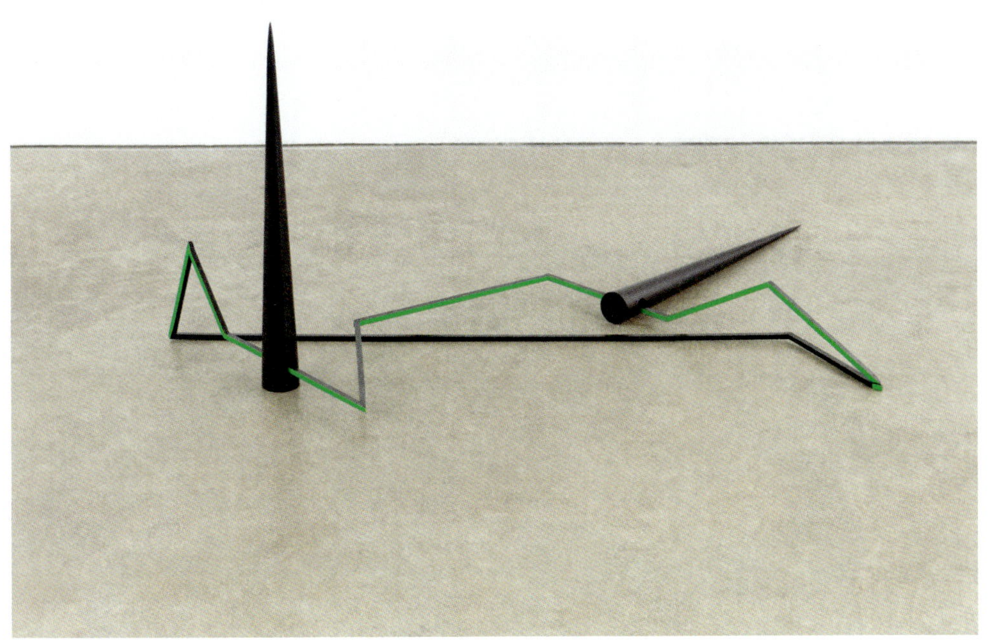

Your Weakness, 2004

LILIANE LIJN

Liliane Lijn was born in New York, studied in Paris and lives in London. She has exhibited internationally since the 1960s, and her work is held in the collections of Tate, the British Museum, the Victoria and Albert Museum and the Art Institute of Chicago, among others. Lijn works across various media – kinetic sculpture, film, text, performance and collage – to explore language, mythology and the relationship between light and matter. She has been the subject of solo exhibitions and presentations at Tate Britain, the Middlesbrough Institute of Modern Art and the Serpentine Gallery. *Converse Column*, a nine-metre-high kinetic text work commissioned by Leeds University, launched in July 2019.

How can one fairly judge the contribution
made by women to the field of modern and
contemporary British sculpture, when there
is still so much art by women to be unveiled?
Every day there is another exhibition of works
by a woman artist, whose work has hardly
been seen for most of her life.

I have lived and worked in London since
1967. I am primarily known for my early kinetic
works, such as *Liquid Reflections* (1966–68),
my series of *Koans* (1969–ongoing), and *Poem
Machines* (1962). Less known are my mature
works: *Cosmic Dramas*, *Conjunction of
Opposites* (1983–86), *Bride* (1988) and *Electric
Bride* (1990). These works have rarely been
seen in the 30 years since I made them. When
these works are shown now, I am asked: how
is it possible that people have been unaware
of this very early, groundbreaking work? All
three installations were made at the end of
the 1980s and spanned the decade in their
development and creation, with numerous
smaller works, drawings and paintings
preceding them. In them, I attempted to
create a new vision of the feminine, going
beyond gender and blending the anthro-
pomorphic with the animal, plant and machine,
connecting kinetics, science and feminism
with archaic myth and the contemplation
of vulnerability and transience.

My large exhibition at the Mead Gallery

in 2005, curated by David Alan Mellor, showed my work up to 1980. In the 1990s and into the early years of the new millennium, I turned inward, exploring my own psyche and the way memory resides in the body. In these intimate works, I use video on very small screens embedded in parts of my body – my elbow, my thigh, my back – to express early childhood memories. Here I think of video as memory both contained and expressed in light. My work is about consciousness, focus, awareness, actually seeing and being in the world.

It is not possible to truly know an artist's work nor their contribution, if that work is not consistently shown over the period of their life. There is still a reinforced glass ceiling blocking museum shows for women artists. Small cracks appear in it, as a few women artists filter through. That ceiling needs to be shattered.

EMMA
PARK

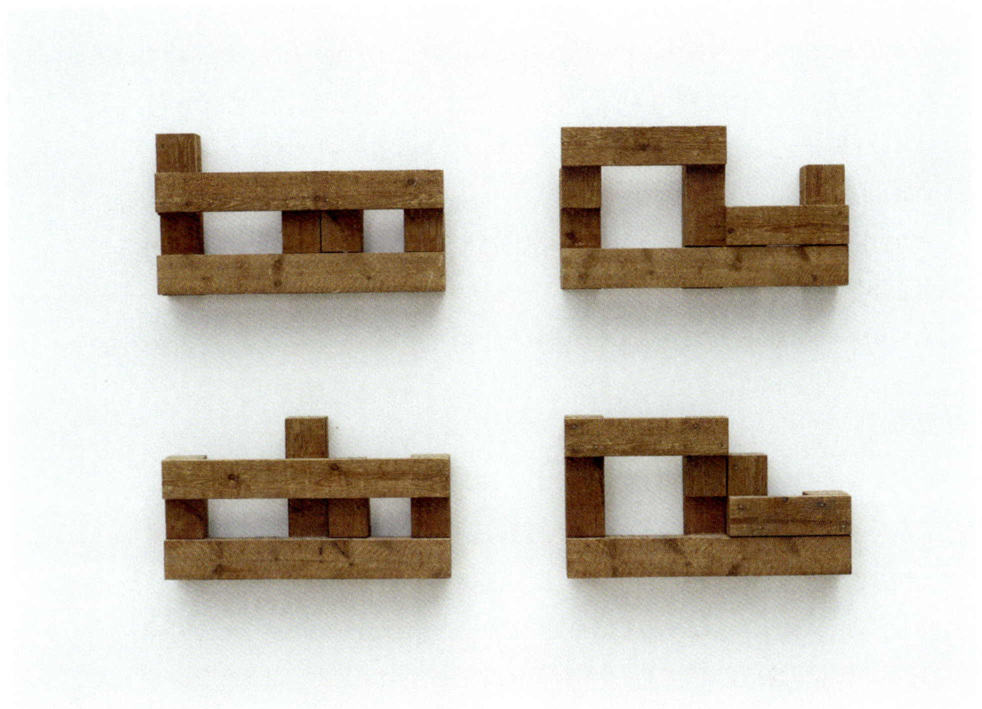

4 Sculptures 'Untitled December 1978', 1978

ALISON
WILDING

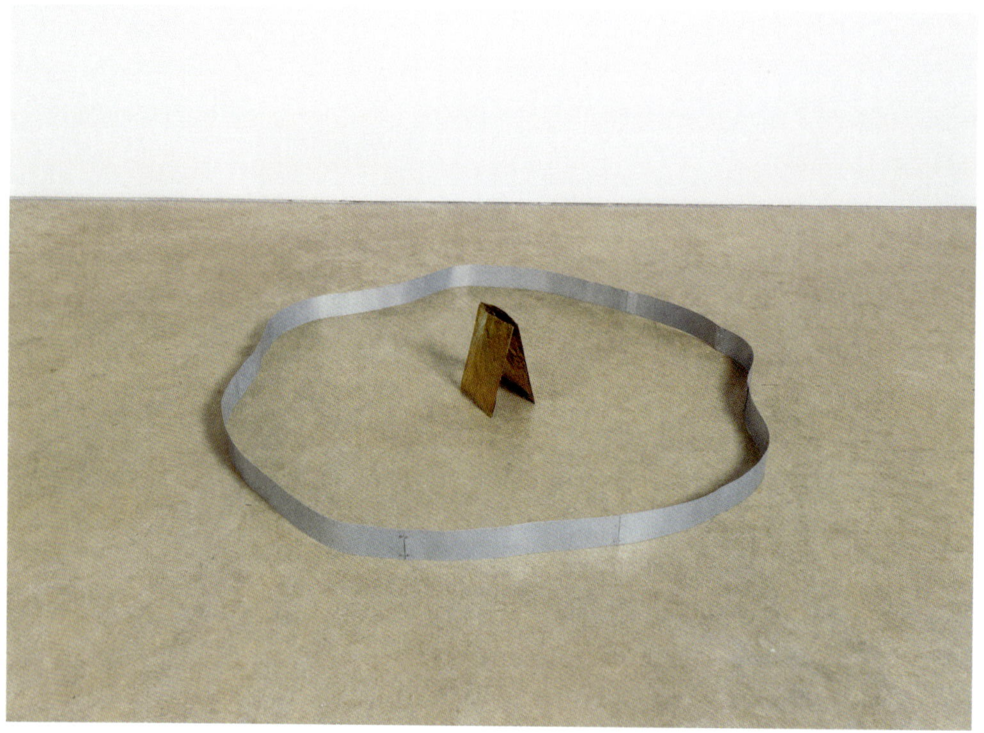

Untitled, 1980

RACHEL
WHITEREAD

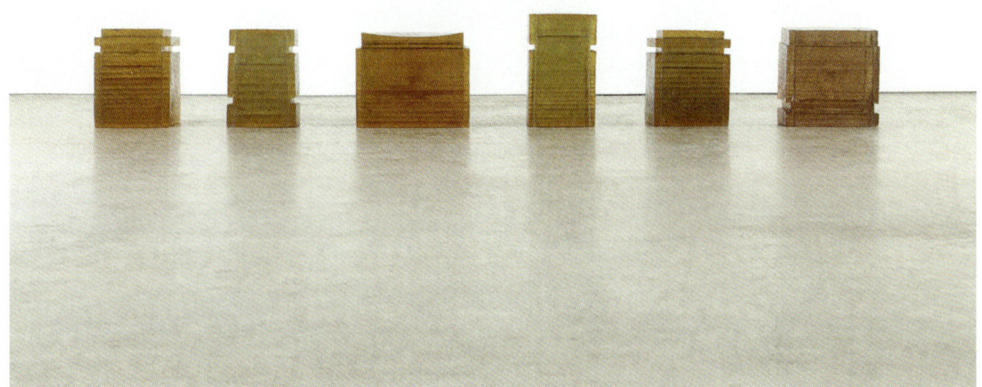

Untitled (6 Spaces), 1994

CLARE LILLEY

Clare Lilley is Director of Programme at Yorkshire Sculpture Park, which was named the UK Art Fund Museum of the Year in 2014. Her curated and published work includes that with Fiona Banner, Lucio Fontana, Damien Hirst, Amar Kanwar, KAWS, Kimsooja, Alfredo Jaar, Shirin Neshat, Giuseppe Penone, Sean Scully, Yinka Shonibare CBE, David Smith, James Turrell, Bill Viola and Ai Weiwei. Since 2012 Clare has curated Frieze Sculpture in Regent's Park, London. She has written for numerous publishers and journals and contributes to conferences, panel discussions and art prizes worldwide. Lilley sits on the Advisory Committee of the Government Art Collection, is an advisor to the HS2 Design Panel and Cavendish Arts Science at Cambridge University and is a trustee of Art UK, London.

Tracey Emin only began working with bronze in the last few years. She will shortly complete building her extensive Margate studio and, in a recent conversation,[1] she spoke about the enormous amount of time and money that is required to create her new sculptures and how this has necessitated both capital investment and a shift in her practice.

Object-sculpture is by its nature materially and spatially assertive, so a sculptor needs logistical and material support as well as the endorsement of others who believe in the undertaking. Unlike many of her peers, Emin receives both from her gallerists, in part because the market supports her value. For many female artists, the complexity of sculpture-making is further complicated by the demands of childbearing and family care, which have an enormous impact on productivity. But so does lack of investment, which could be equated to lack of belief, since dealers and collectors are both predominantly male and tend to invest in that with which they are familiar and upon which they can realise return.

Women contribute hugely to the nuance of sculpture-making, offering much and including a sensibility that Barbara Hepworth defined thus: 'It may be that the sensation of being a woman presents yet another facet of the sculptural idea.'[2] However, women sculptors number far fewer than men and they have less power within the industry. Search online for 'British women sculptors' and Wikipedia throws out a blindingly incomplete and meagre list in comparison to a 'male' search; make a similar online search for 'most important or successful artist' of any gender and the results are dominated by painters, highlighting the particular difficulties of making sculpture as well as its market status.

In this respect, Cathy de Monchaux has cited Virginia Woolf's 1929 essay 'A Room of One's Own' in which Woolf explores the social, political and financial conditions required for women's creativity (and from today's perspective highlighting only modest progression over almost a century), as inspiration for her sculpture, *Beyond Thinking* (2018).[3] In effect, even nowadays fewer women receive the investment required for making sculpture, a phenomenon that *artnet* recently termed the 'bronze ceiling'.[4] The Mei Moses index shows how secondary sales by some female artists are currently accelerating at a rate of knots but women artists still only represent two per cent of the auction market,[5] and museum acquisitions of work by women trail dismally behind those of men.[6] Through this prism, we see that women artists are being asked to prove themselves primarily through the realisable gain of a male-dominated marketplace. Hepworth was an extraordinary trailblazer but it is only in recent years that her market value has come into line with her closest associate, Henry Moore.

There is still a long way to go, but I pay tribute to the many inspiring British women whose art and whose tenacity so boldly defy the restrictions of the current art market.

1   Tracey Emin and Clare Lilley in conversation during the installation of Emin's *When I Sleep* (2018), for Frieze Sculpture 2019, July 2019

2   Barbara Hepworth quoted in Herbert Read, 'Introduction', in Barbara Hepworth: Carvings and Drawings (London: Lund Humphries, 1952), facing plate 135

3   Louise Buck, 'Quietly disturbing the status quo' Art Agency, Partners, 8 November 2020, www.artagencypartners. com/louisa-buck-must-see-1-november-2018/ [accessed 19 February 2020]

4   Amah-Rose Abrams, 'The Bronze Ceiling? What the Gender Gap in Public Sculpture Tells Us About the Barriers for Women in Art', *artnet,* 1 August 2019, news.artnet. com/art-world/publicsculpture-gender-gap-1603633 [accessed 19 February 2020]

5   Charlotte Burns and Julia Halperin, 'Female Artists Represent Just 2 Percent of the Market. Here's Why—and How That Can Change', *artnet*, 19 September 2018, news.artnet.com/womens-place-in-theart-world/female-artists-representjust-just-2-percent-market-heres-can-change-1654954 [accessed 19 February 2020]

6   Charlotte Burns and Julia Halperin, Art Agency, Partners, 'Museum Acquisitions of Work by Women Peaked a Decade Ago—and Have Stalled Since', 19 September 2019, www. artagencypartners.com/women-study-museums/?utmcampaign=AAP_19_Sept &utmcontent=aap_19_sept_julia_vennitti &utmmedium=email&utm_source=zaius [accessed 19 February 2020]

SHIRAZEH
HOUSHIARY

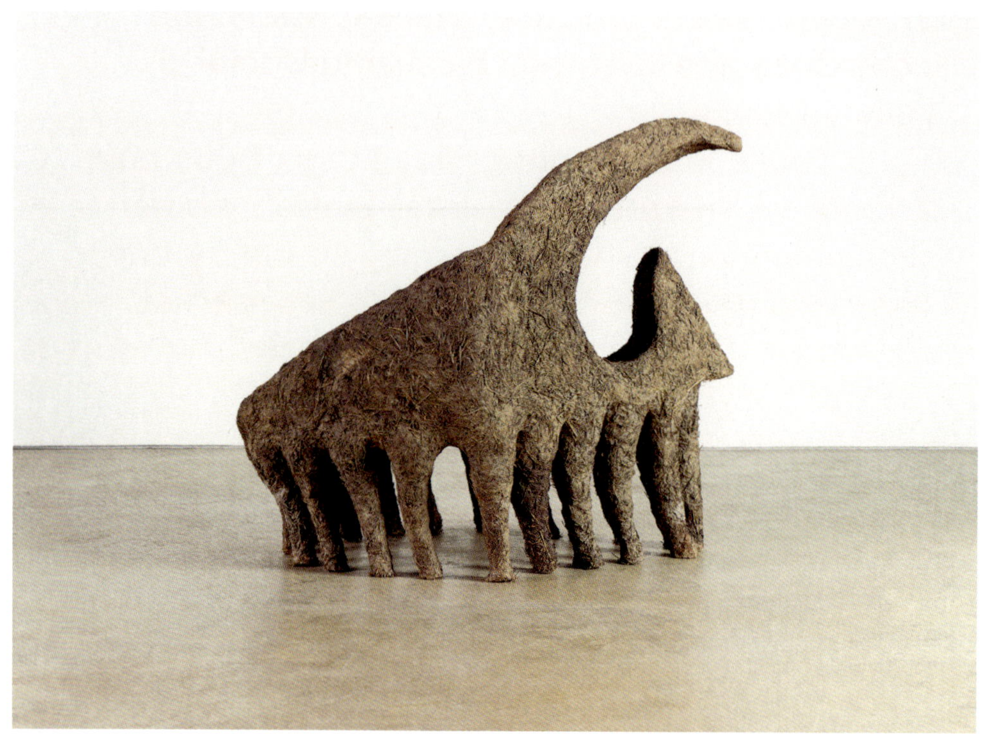

Listen to the Tale of the Reed No. 3, 1982

ELISABETH
FRINK

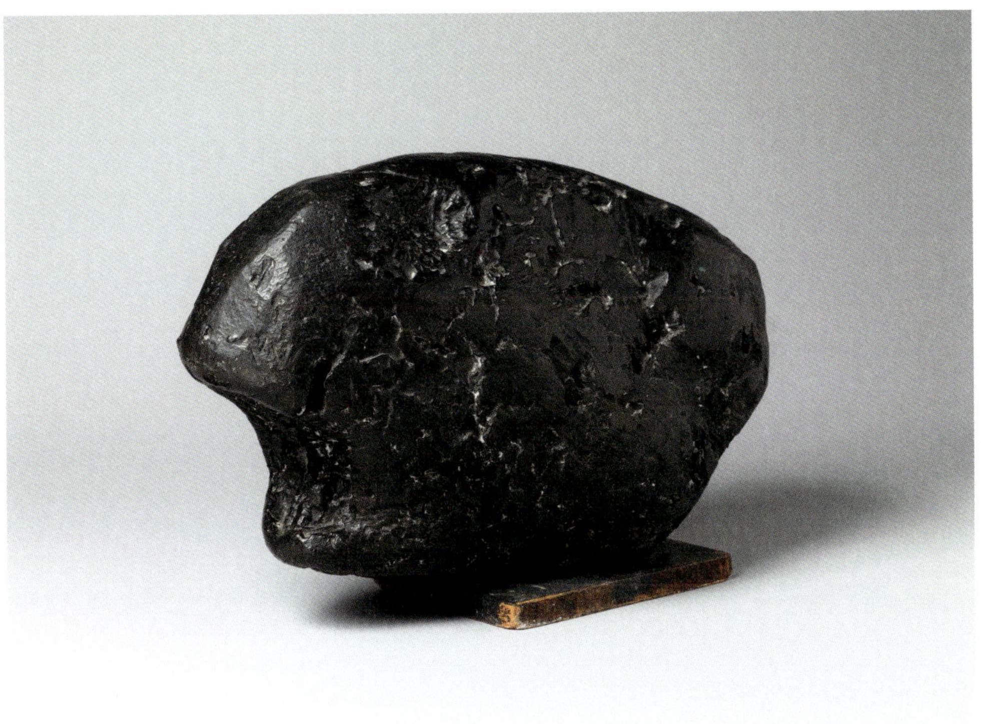

Head, 1959

SHELAGH
CLUETT

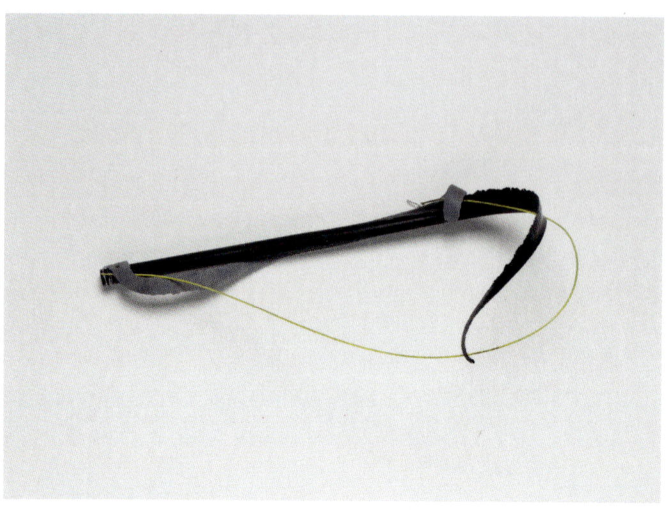

KATHERINE
GILI

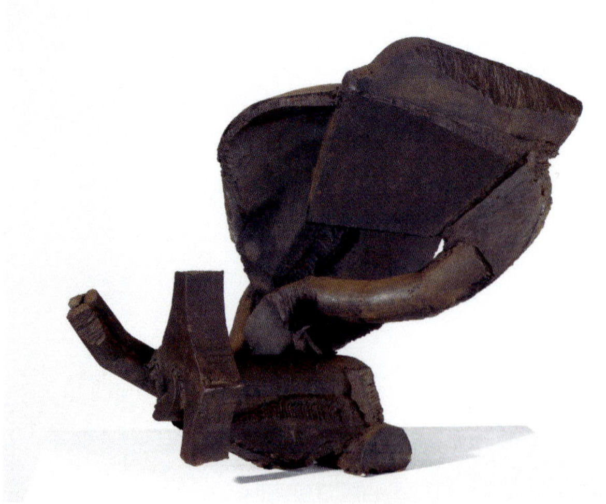

Untitled, c. 1981 (top); *Pistil*, 1979 (bottom)

MARGARET ORGAN

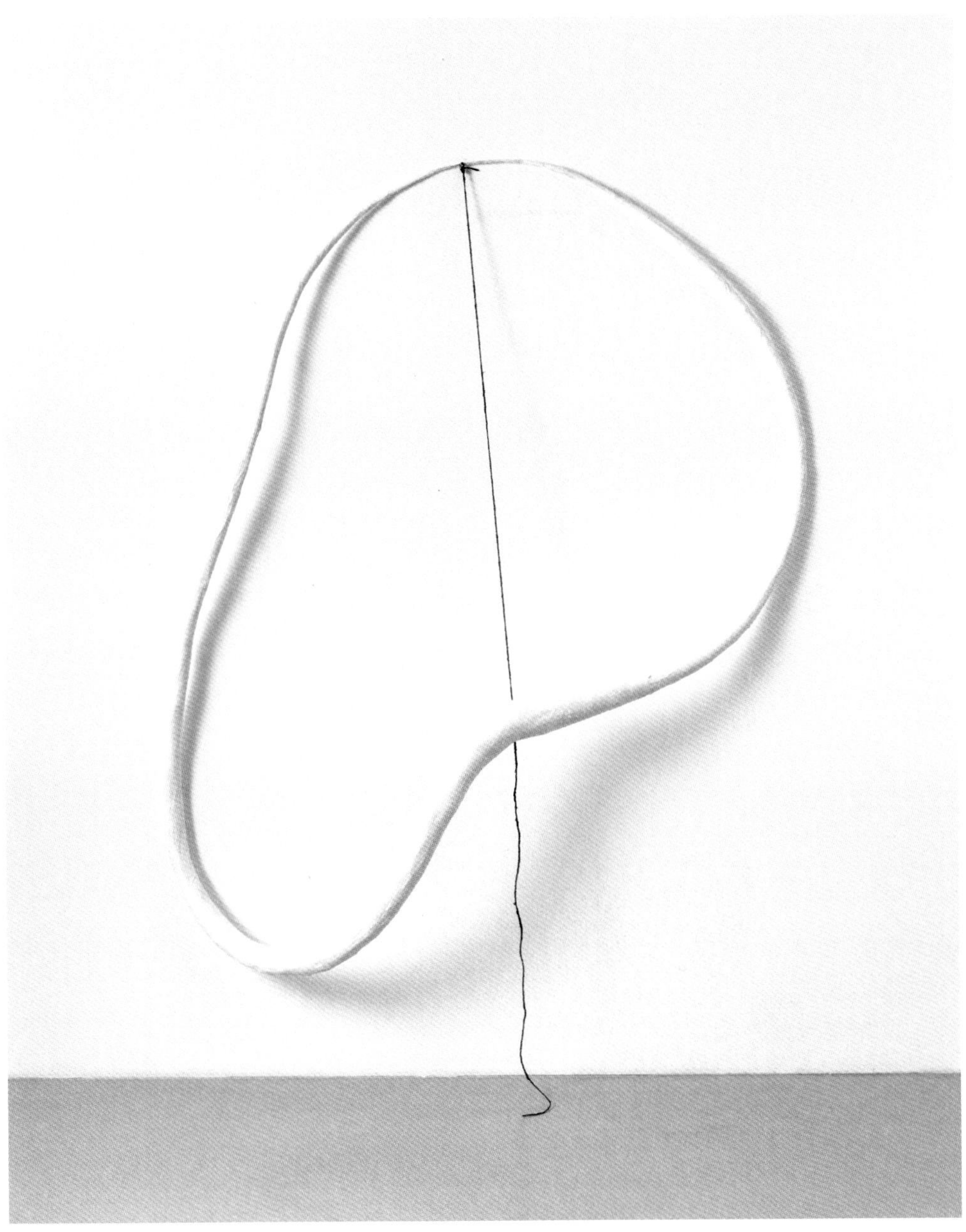

Loop, 1978/2014

ROSANNE ROBERTSON

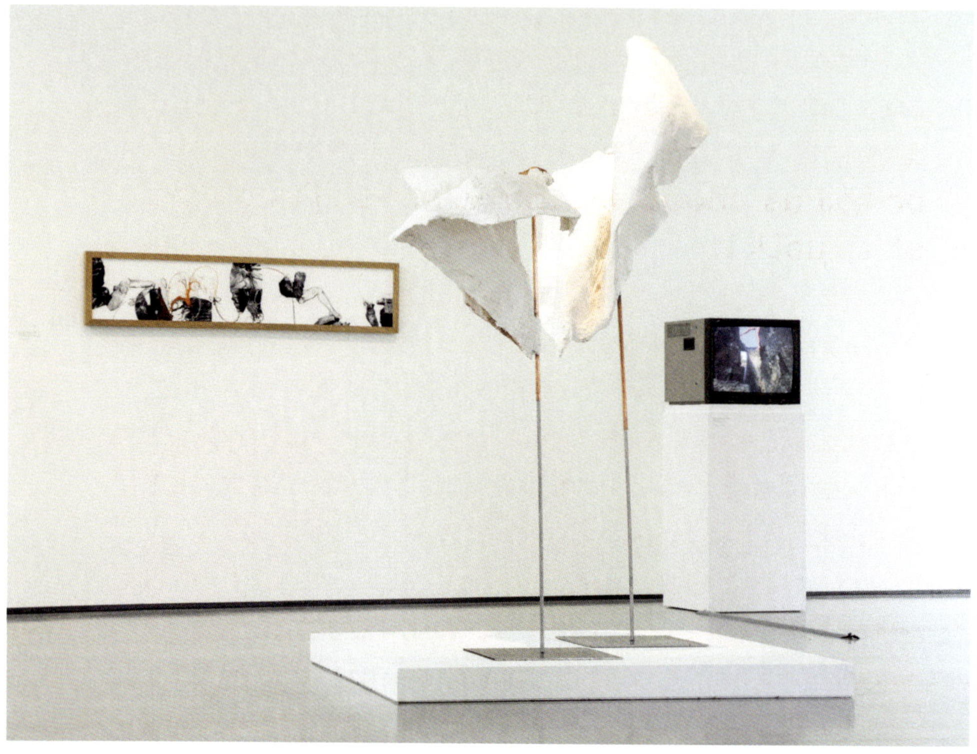

Rosanne Robertson was born in Sunderland in 1984. Their practice spans sculpture, photography, drawing and performance to explore the boundaries of the human body and its environment. Robertson's body of works titled *Stone (Butch)* was exhibited as a contemporary intervention within the display of work by Barbara Hepworth at The Hepworth Wakefield in 2019 and in the group exhibition *Associated Matter* at Yorkshire Scupture Park as part of Yorkshire Sculpture International 2019. Their public sculpture *We Built Ships* (2020) was commissioned by Sunderland Council as a legacy to the 700 women who worked in the city's shipyards. Their work has been included in reviews and articles in *Elephant*, *Wallpaper* and the *Financial Times*.

The phrase 'set in stone' has traditionally represented the idea of being complete and static. Representations of the figure in sculpture, standing as bodies of stone punctuating history, have often told a singular and narrow story about gender and sexuality, a single understanding which does not show or tell us about another ever-shifting kind of situation.

A much queerer situation.

Stone (Butch) is a body of work I began as a Yorkshire Sculpture International Associate Artist. The title introduces the act of connecting the qualities of stone, water and other aspects of nature with our gender expressions, sexuality and identity. The term *stone butch* is taken from butch lesbian and trans activist Leslie Feinberg's novel *Stone Butch Blues* (1993). It is a term that has been popularised since the early 1990s and is used to describe a masculine gender expression in butch and lesbian identity:

'The cops picked out the most stone butch of them all to destroy with humiliation, a woman everyone said, "wore a raincoat in the shower."' [1]

It is this raincoat layer, thick skin or barrier that I am interested in as a terrain, and this is the terrain of the *Stone (Butch)* works. It is the dark spaces in the margins and cracks that I aim to transcend.

 Stone (Butch) focuses on a journey I made to a set of stones called the Bridestones that are situated above Todmorden in the Upper Calder Valley, West Yorkshire. I took plaster casts of cracks in the stones to make sculptures which I titled *chasmschism* (2019). This process of casting directly from the cracked stones turns a negative space into a positive one, to see what that feels and looks like. I see the sculptures as active forms in a raw state which belong to both the landscape and the body at the same time.

 Other works include *stonebodywater* (2019), which is a video of a bodily intervention I carried out in white underwear and sport socks packed with mulch under a fast-flowing waterway. I also created drawings of body parts linking photographs of the Bridestones in two fluid and wide-scale compositions. *Stone (Butch)* was exhibited across two exhibitions during Yorkshire Sculpture International 2019, at *Associated Matter* at Yorkshire Sculpture Park and as a contemporary intervention within the display of Barbara Hepworth's work at The Hepworth Wakefield.

 These works explore the queer body within the landscape and reclaim a natural space for queer and butch identity from

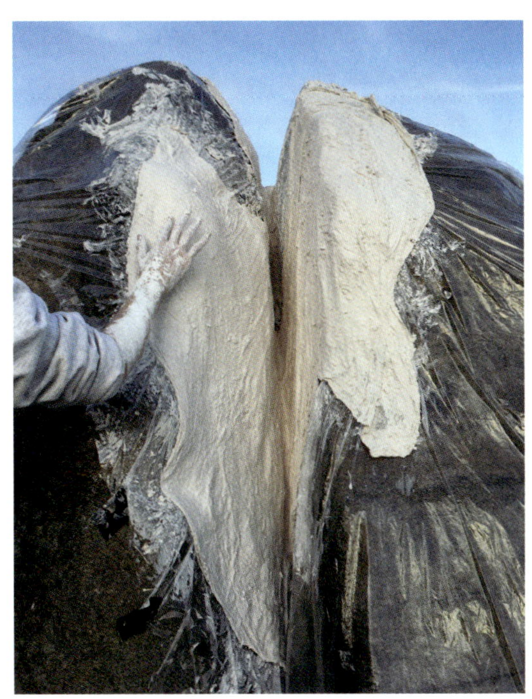

a violent history of being deemed 'against nature'. I saw the natural stone formations as queer forms and changing bodies that are not set in stone, but revealed to us over a long period of time, as fluid structures shaped by water and erosion. These queer bodies are as fluid as the water that shapes them and as plural as the grains of sand that erode them.

1   Leslie Feinberg, *Stone Butch Blues*
     (Alyson Books: New York, 2004 [1993]), p. 6

Stone (Butch), 2019, installation view at The Hepworth Wakefield, 2019 (p. 86);
Making *chasmschism*, 2019 (this page)

ROSE
FINN-KELCEY

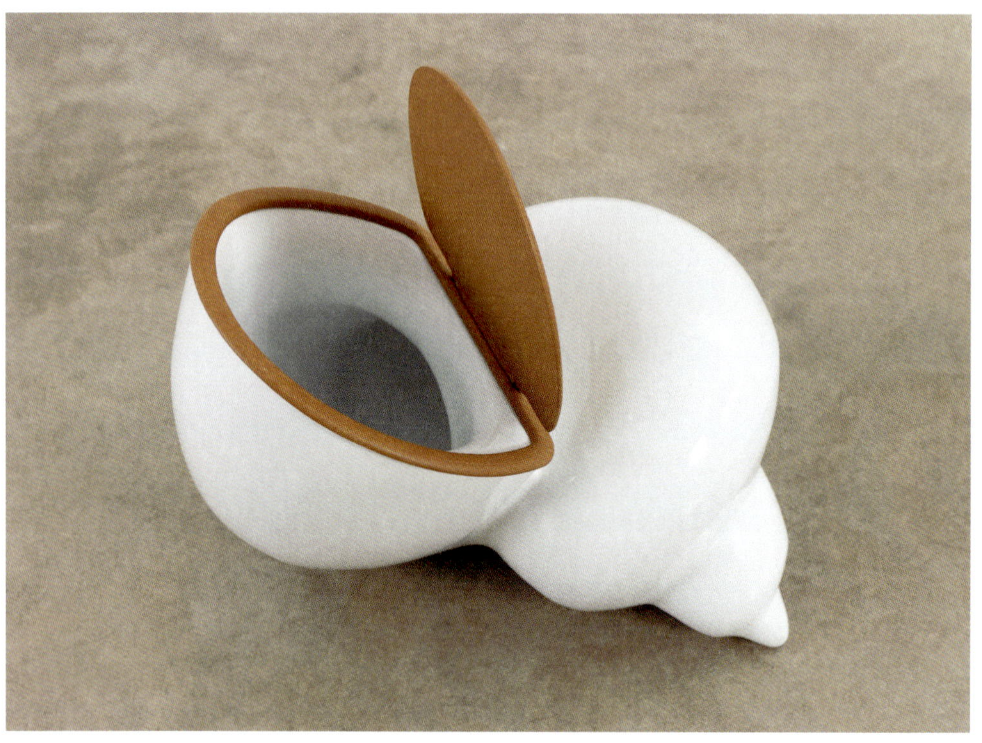

God's Bog, 2001

CORNELIA PARKER

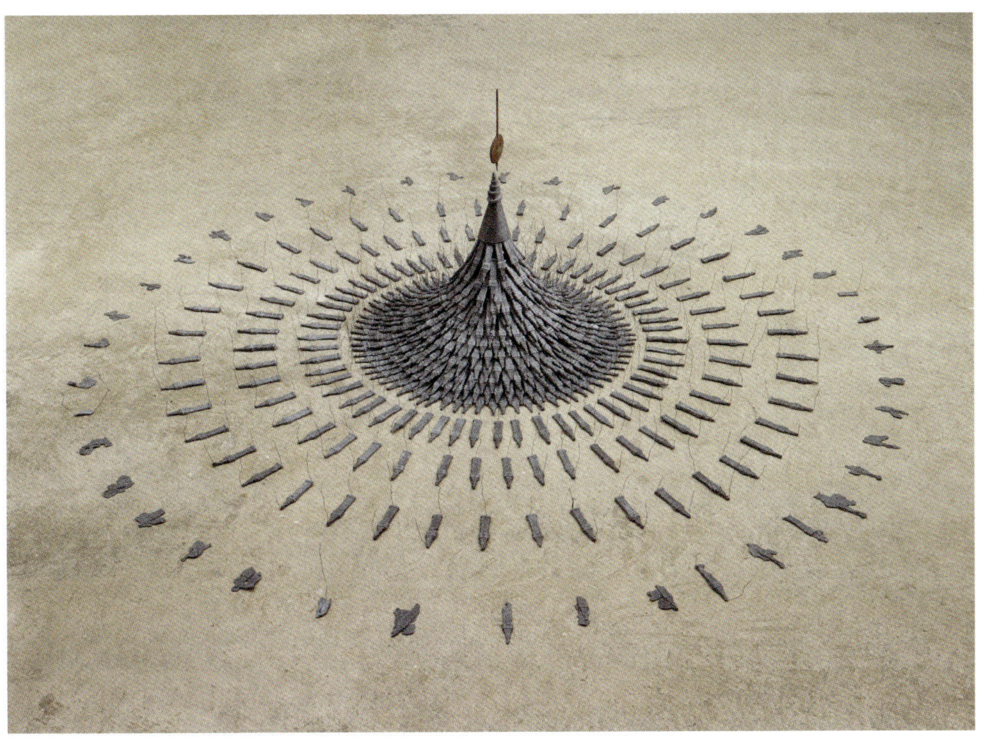

Fleeting Monument, 1985

WENDY
TAYLOR

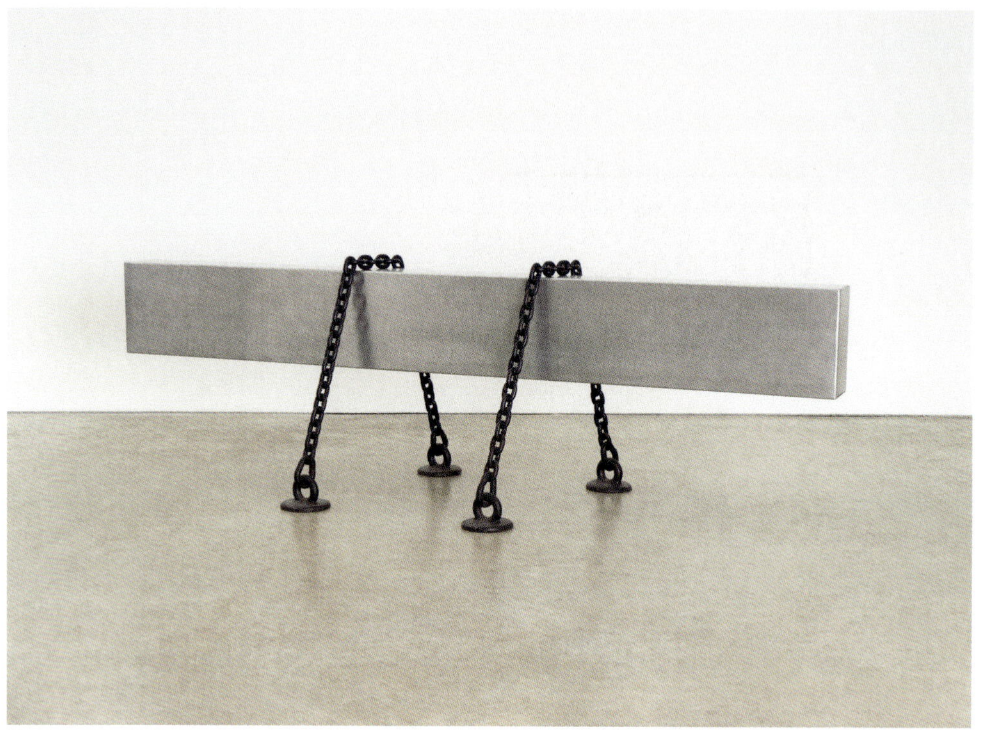

Inversion, 1970

MEG
RUTHERFORD

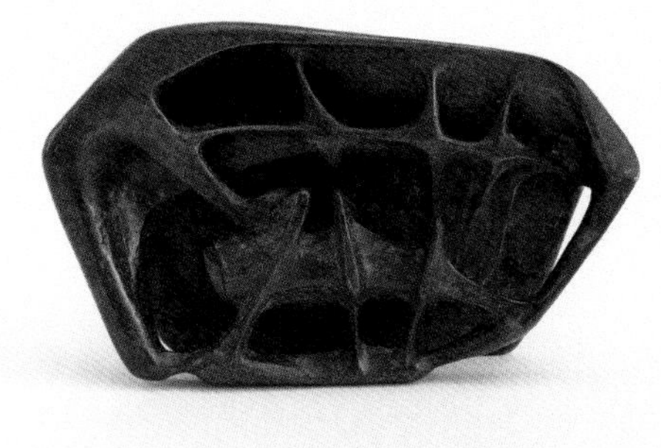

LYGIA
CLARK

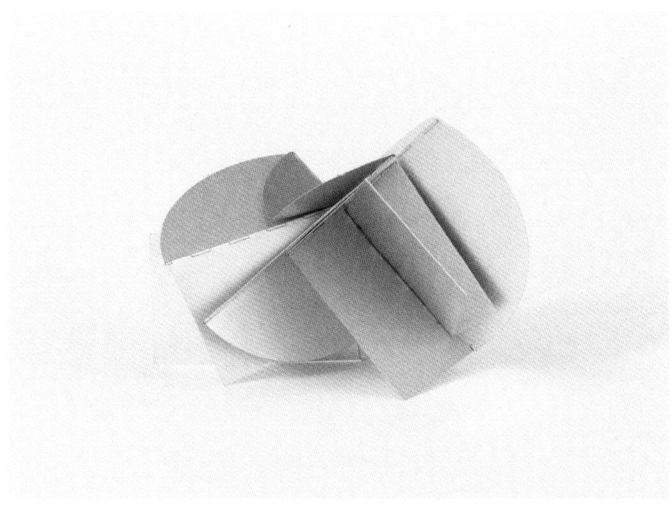

Quartros, 1960 (top); *Animal 3*, 1969 (bottom)

VERONICA RYAN

Veronica Ryan was born in 1956 on the Caribbean island of Montserrat, raised and educated in England, and now divides her time between New York City and the UK. Ryan's evocative sculptures and installations employ a wide range of materials, including bronze, plaster, marble, textiles and found objects, and a similar breadth of processes, from casting and carving to stitching, modelling and assembling. Much of her work draws on personal memories and experiences, making connections across time and place, and reflecting the wider psychological implications of history, trauma and recovery. Her work is held in various public and private collections and has featured in solo exhibitions at key galleries and museums including Camden Arts Centre, London; Kettle's Yard, Cambridge; Castlefield Gallery, Manchester; the Aldrich Contemporary Art Museum, Ridgefield, Connecticut; the Mattress Factory, Pittsburgh and at Paula Cooper Gallery in New York. In 2018 Ryan was awarded the Freelands Award from the Freelands Foundation; a major solo exhibition will take place at Spike Island, Bristol in autumn 2020.

The 1980s seemed a time of immense forward movement, but there is no place for complacency in spite of more female visibility. Statistics show that essential movement forward cannot be taken for granted. There have been significant shifts, but fundamental structures and systems need constant examining. Psychological subtexts and paradigms are harder to shift.

Passion and a need to work are essential criteria for artistic practice; and proactive engagement remains vital to personal endeavour. Crucial moments come around, including pivotal exhibitions, and the support of a few individuals both from galleries and by patronage matters.

Early on in school and college, my awareness of documented female artists included (other than some Bauhaus women artists by default) Camille Claudel, Elisabeth Frink, Barbara Hepworth, Eva Hesse, Hannah Höch, Gwen John and Germaine Richier, among others. And ironically, it was while looking up the male artists for essays that one became aware, residually, of these women artists. Thames & Hudson's book *African Art: An Introduction* by Frank Willett (1971) was a taster. Discovering the bookshop New Beacon Books in Finsbury Park as an undergraduate at Corsham Court was pivotal. I remember Betye Saar; her work appeared very different

from my experience of art at an early age.
The art teachers at school were very
supportive; I remember carving chalk in
response to Barbara Hepworth well before
doing any exams.

Later on, I was very pleased to have
access to established women artists: Phyllida
Barlow, Louise Bourgeois, Isa Genzken, Maren
Hassinger, Carmen Herrera, Alison Wilding,
Yayoi Kusama, Agnes Martin and Senga Nengudi.
Too many to name. I remember spending a lot
of time in the Egyptian section of the British
Museum, as a postgraduate Slade student,
which was wonderful.

Residencies have been continually
paramount. Being awarded an Acme House in
Leyton soon after leaving the Slade, as well as
some early involvement with the Whitechapel
London Open and residency programmes in
education in local schools, were crucial to my
early career as an artist. My experiences and
my specific practice led me to value education
as essential, introducing ongoing criteria for
understanding early interventions, later
commitment, and passion in communities.

SOKARI
DOUGLAS CAMP

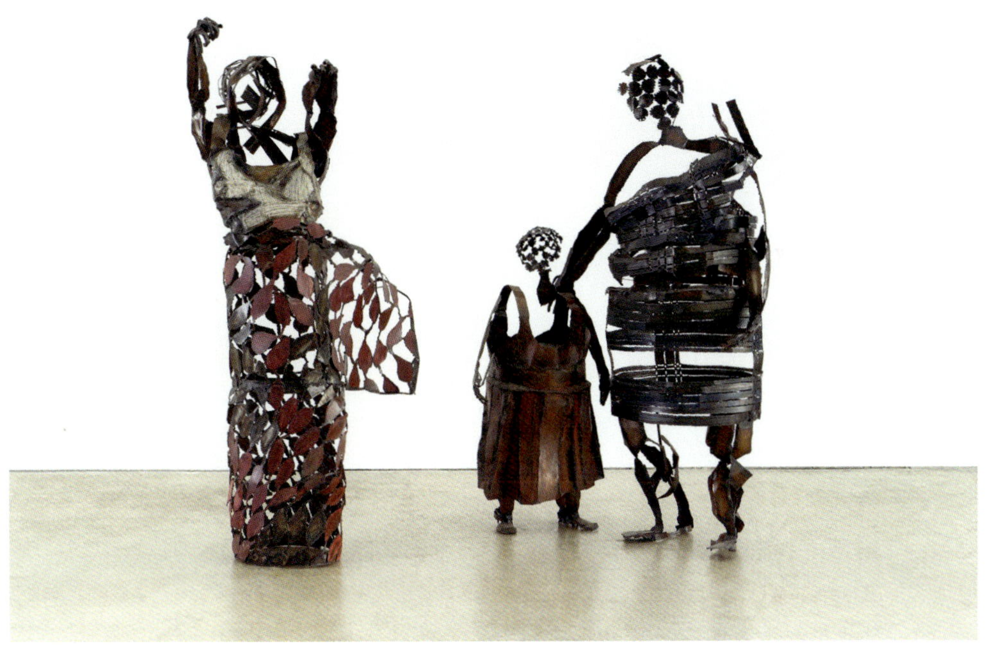

Audience (from *Show Boat, Alali Aru* installation), 1986

LUCIA NOGUEIRA

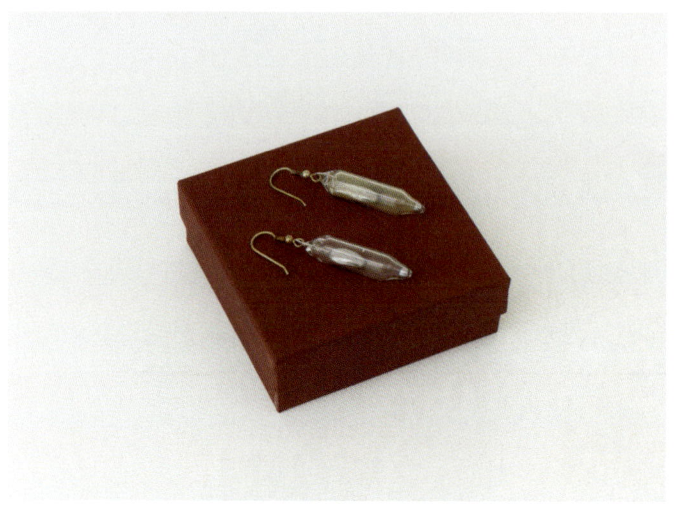

SHELAGH WAKELY

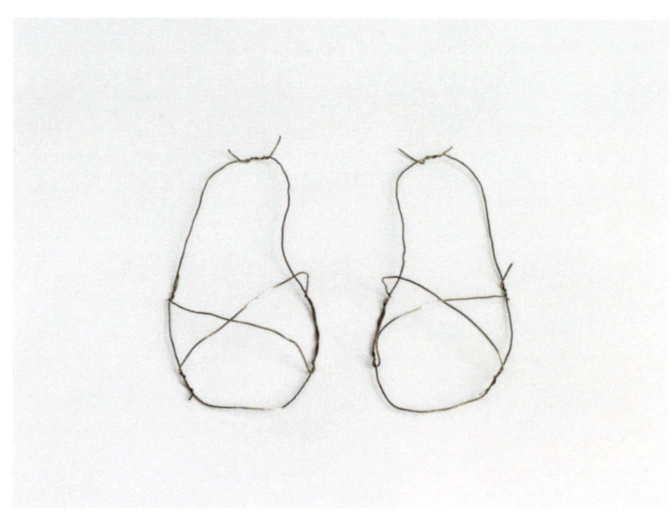

One and Three, 1994 (top); *Sine Qua Non*, 1982 (bottom)

PERMINDAR
KAUR

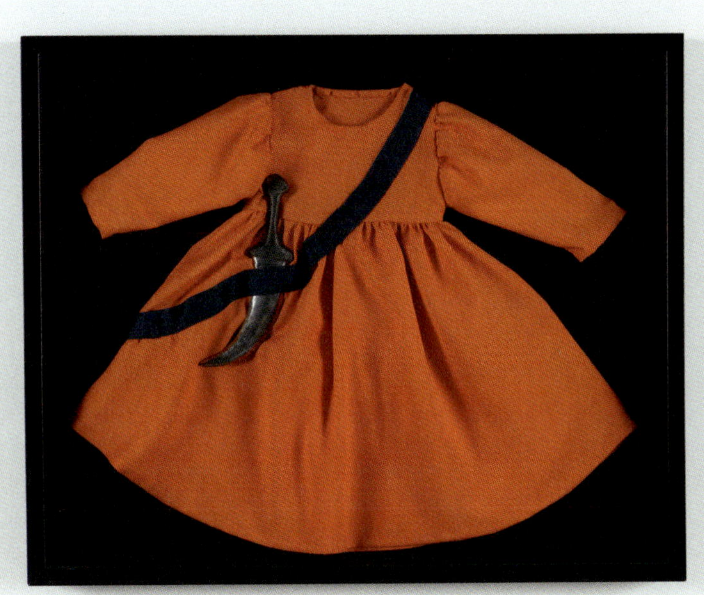

Innocence, 1993

JOY SLEEMAN

Joy Sleeman is Professor of Art History and Theory at UCL Slade School of Fine Art where she has taught these subjects since 1995. She was Henry Moore Fellow in the History of Sculpture in the History of Art Department at UCL (1996–97) and, since 2015, Visiting Professor of the History of Sculpture at the University of Lincoln. Sleeman writes, curates and lectures on aspects of land art and sculpture for art galleries, museums and other arts organisations as well as in academic contexts. She was on the editorial board of the *Sculpture Journal* from 2000 to 2019 and is a member of AICA (International Association of Art Critics).

'Why are there so few women in your exhibition?' This, or variations on it, was a recurrent question posed to me during the tour of the exhibition that I co-curated for the Arts Council Collection in 2013–14, *Uncommon Ground: Land Art in Britain 1966–1979*.

In curating *Uncommon Ground* I realised that we were presenting an exhibition that was itself a history of exhibitions. I found investigating exhibition histories revealing of the roles, appearances and disappearances of women and art by women.

There was one woman in the list of artists (Susan Hiller), four more who made or co-authored work that was shown at every venue, including in a film screening (Georgia Boyle, Rita Donagh, Joan Hills, Jenny Okun) and a work recovered and restored during the run of the tour and shown only at the last venue, by Phillippa Ecobichon. The work of Marie Yates was discussed in the catalogue.[1]

Work by Ecobichon and Yates had already featured in group exhibitions of vanguard landscape art in the 1970s, notably *Artists Over Land* at the Arnolfini in Bristol (1975) and *An Element of Landscape* (1974), selected by Jeremy Rees and containing work purchased for the Arts Council Collection. In these exhibitions, work by Ecobichon and Yates had been shown alongside work by men who went on to be much better known in this field, men who were also represented in *Uncommon Ground*, for example Hamish Fulton, Richard Long and Bruce McLean.

Researching *The New Art* exhibition at the Hayward Gallery in 1972, I became fascinated by what went on around the exhibition, as well as what was included in it (and there were no women exhibiting).[2] Two women featured prominently in that history: Anne Seymour who was the selector of the exhibition (the word 'curator' was not yet in common use) and the Chairman [sic.] of the Artists' Union, artist Mary Kelly, who proposed and helped stage a representation of the Union outside the exhibition's entrance. A few years later, representation outside the Hayward Gallery turned to protest, according to Griselda Pollock, at the lack of inclusion of work by women in *The Condition of Sculpture* exhibition in 1975.[3] There were five women in this exhibition and 36 men. Incidentally, several other women were considered for inclusion in the exhibition and were left out by the curator/selector, sculptor William Tucker, for reasons apparently including that he no longer considered their work to be sculpture or that they were too old (Tucker included only artists 'under the age of about 40'). These variables – definitions of what sculpture is, and of age – as well as gender have impacted historically on the inclusion or exclusion of women in exhibitions of sculpture.

I have come to realise that exhibitions are not the end point of a process. Exhibitions start things, and they begin processes of change and reassessment. They don't close a chapter but open it.

1   *Uncommon Ground: Land Art in Britain 1966–1979*, (London: Hayward Publishing), 2013. 24 artists and artist groups are listed and have individual artist entries in the catalogue

2   Joy Sleeman, 'The New Art Hayward Gallery London 1972: new as compromise or when what happens around the exhibition is as interesting as what happens in the exhibition', *Sculpture Journal*, 21.2 (2012), pp. 63–74

3   Griselda Pollock, 'Feminism, Femininity and the Hayward Annual Exhibition 1978', *Feminist Review*, No. 2 (1979), pp. 33–55

CHRONOLOGY

1946

The Arts Council Collection is formed.

1947

Arts Council Collection purchases its first work by a sculptor: Barbara Hepworth's drawing *Reconstruction* (1947).

1949

Simone de Beauvoir's *The Second Sex* is published. This text is often considered the starting point of second-wave feminism.

1952

The British Pavilion at the Venice Biennale exhibits the work of a generation of sculptors who emerged after the Second World War. The sharp, distorted, supernatural forms used by this all-male cohort prompts art historian Herbert Read to coin the term *Geometry of Fear*.

1953

Arts Council Collection purchases its first sculpture by Elisabeth Frink, *Bird* (1952), while she is still a student at Chelsea School of Art.

1958

Arts Council Collection purchases its first Barbara Hepworth sculpture, *Icon* (1957).

Barbara Hepworth is appointed CBE.

1965

Barbara Hepworth is appointed DBE.

1967

The introduction of the Abortion Act legalises abortion in the UK and standardises the tax-paid provision of the service on the NHS, giving women more control over their futures.

1968

The self-titled *Barbara Hepworth* retrospective opens at the Tate Gallery (now Tate Britain) displaying works from her early carvings through to more recent metal works. Hepworth also directs the exhibition design, rejecting neutral painted plinths in favour of bespoke concrete ones accompanied by pot plants, invoking ideas of domesticity.

1950

Barbara Hepworth represents Britain at Venice Biennale, two years after Henry Moore.

1951

The Festival of Britain is mounted to mark the centenary of the Great Exhibition of 1851. The festival, occupying numerous sites and centred on the South Bank, features works by Mitzi Cunliffe, Daphne Hardy, Barbara Hepworth and Karin Jonzen, among many others.

The Arts Council Collection purchases its first sculpture by a woman artist: Karin Jonzen's *Seated Nude*.

1959

Barbara Hepworth is the first British artist to win the São Paulo Biennale Grand Prix.

1961

The contraceptive pill becomes available on the NHS for the first time, giving women unprecedented control over their reproductive choices.

1964

The Married Women's Property Act revision entitles women to half of any savings from the allowance given to them by their husbands upon separation, giving stay-at-home women more independence and security.

1970

Allen Jones's fibreglass fetish mannequins, *Hatstand*, *Table* and *Chair* (1969) debut at Tooth Gallery, London, to feminist protests focusing on the works' perceived misogyny and exploitation of women which continue upon subsequent showings.

Germaine Greer's *The Female Eunuch* is published – a key text in 1970s feminism which explores the idea that traditional consumerist and familial systems repress female sexuality.

Women Artists 1550–1950, curated by Ann Sutherland Harris and Linda Nochlin, opens at Los Angeles County Museum of Art.

British Sculpture Out of the Sixties, selected by American art critic Gene Baro, opens at the ICA, showing 16 artists including only one woman, Kim Lim.

1971

Linda Nochlin's pioneering essay 'Why Have There Been No Great Women Artists?' is published. The text investigates the institutional barriers experienced by women in the arts, and is a landmark work in feminist art and its theory.

1972

Womanhouse, the first exhibition of avowedly feminist work by contemporary artists is organised by Judy Chicago and Miriam Schapiro in a dilapidated mansion in Los Angeles. It features their students from California Institute of the Arts' (CalArts) Feminist Art Program as well as local women artists.

Rosie Boycott and Marsha Rowe found feminist magazine *Spare Rib*.

The New Art opens at Hayward Gallery, the first institutional survey of British conceptual art, curated by Anne Seymour. It comes under scrutiny for representing no female artists.

1975

Barbara Hepworth dies in a fire at her St Ives studio on 20 May.

The Condition of Sculpture opens at the Hayward Gallery. Curated by the sculptor William Tucker, the exhibition features the work of 37 men and four women.

Women and Work opens at South London Art Gallery, documenting the new problems faced by female employees of a South London metal box factory following the Equal Pay Act. The show features the work of Mary Kelly, Margaret Harrison and Kay Hunt.

The Pregnancy and Discrimination Act is passed to prohibit discrimination on the basis of pregnancy, childbirth or related medical conditions.

The Equal Pay Act, the Sex Discrimination Act and the Employment Protection Act all come into effect to legislate for parity in the workplace and prohibit less favourable treatment based on gender or marital status.

1978

In response to the gender imbalance in its 1977 exhibition, the *Hayward Annual '78* has an all-female selection committee (Gillian Wise Ciobotaru, Rita Donagh, Tess Jaray, Liliane Lijn and Kim Lim) and becomes known as the 'women's annual' despite also featuring work by men.

1979

Judy Chicago completes her hugely influential large-scale feminist installation *The Dinner Party*, featuring handmade place settings for 39 historical and mythical famous women.

Eva Hesse: Sculpture opens at Whitechapel Gallery, the first major survey of Hesse's work in the UK.

Margaret Thatcher becomes Britain's first female Prime Minister.

British Sculpture '72 opens at the Royal Academy showing works by 24 artists, all male.

1974

Feminist art group S.L.A.G. (South London Art Group) transform 14 Radnor Terrace in Lambeth, South London, into a large-scale installation, *A Woman's Place*, critiquing family life, heavily influenced by Judy Chicago and Miriam Schapiro's *Womanhouse*, Los Angeles.

1976

Lucy Lippard's *From the Centre: Feminist Essays on Women's Work* is published.

The Barbara Hepworth Museum and Gardens opens at her former studio in St Ives.

The Domestic Violence and Matrimonial Proceedings Act is established to give more equal rights and protection to married women.

1977

Yorkshire Sculpture Park is founded on Bretton Hall's 500-acre site spanning South and West Yorkshire – the UK's first sculpture park, adopting the 'gallery without walls' approach.

MaMa: Women Artists Together is published, a booklet of articles and information on and by women artists working in Britain.

1980

ACME Gallery, London, launches *Eight Artists: Women*. Part 1 (3–25 October) features Shelagh Cluett, Emma Park, Jozefa Rogocki and Claire Smith, and Part 2 (31 October–22 November) shows Mikey Cuddihy, Sarah Greengrass, Margaret Organ and Alison Wilding.

1981

bell hooks' *Ain't I A Woman: Black Women and Feminism* is published. It examines the effect of sexism and racism on black women, feminist movements and the civil rights movement.

1982

The Women Artists' Slide Library starts in London in order to establish documentation of women's work.

Elisabeth Frink is appointed DBE.

1983

The Sculpture Show, the largest exhibition of living sculptors to have been shown in Britain at the time, opens at the Hayward Gallery and the Serpentine Gallery. Curated by the sculptors Paul de Monchaux and Kate Blacker, and the curator and writer Fenella Crichton, the exhibition features the work of 36 men, 11 women and one mixed collective.

Sculpture by Women opens at Ikon, Birmingham, exhibiting Elona Bennett, Sheila Clayton, Janet Hedges, Cornelia Parker and Lois Williams.

5 Black Women Artists Living in Britain opens at the Africa Centre, London, curated by Lubaina Himid.

Black Woman Time Now exhibition opens at Battersea Arts Centre, curated by Lubaina Himid.

1987

Helen Chadwick is nominated for the Turner Prize. Richard Deacon wins.

A Quiet Revolution: British Sculpture since 1965 tours the United States, curated by Mary Jane Jacob and organised by Chicago Museum of Contemporary Art and the San Francisco Museum of Modern Art. It represents just six artists, all men: Tony Cragg, Richard Deacon, Barry Flanagan, Richard Long, David Nash and Bill Woodrow.

In the UK, Diane Abbott becomes the first black woman to be elected to the House of Commons.

1988

Alison Wilding is nominated for the Turner Prize. Tony Cragg wins.

Freeze opens in an empty London Port Authority building at Surrey Docks. Organised by Damien Hirst and featuring work by 16 young artists, this exhibition is considered pivotal in the development of the Young British Art (YBA) scene.

1993

Bad Girls, curated by Kate Bush, Emma Dexter and Nicola White, opens at the ICA, embracing the playful, bold and humorous work of six British and American women: Helen Chadwick, Dorothy Cross, Nicole Eisenman, Rachel Evans, Nan Goldin and Sue Williams.

Rachel Whiteread is the first female artist to win the Turner Prize. *House,* Whiteread's cast of the last-standing building yet to be knocked down on Wennington Green is unveiled and prompts national debate around contemporary art and public welfare, before being demolished 80 days later in early 1994.

Tate St Ives opens, exhibiting work by modern British artists connected to the Cornwall coast, and managing the Barbara Hepworth Museum and Sculpture Garden.

Gravity & Grace: The Changing Condition of Sculpture 1965–1975 opens at Hayward Gallery and includes the work of only one female artist, Eva Hesse, among that of 19 men.

Equality between women and men in higher education enrolment numbers is reached.

1985

Guerrilla Girls, an anonymous group of feminist women artists, forms in New York with the aim of raising awareness of and tackling gender and racial inequality in the arts.

The Thin Black Line opens at the ICA – an exhibition of black women artists curated by Lubaina Himid.

1986

Third Generation: Women Sculptors Today opens at various sites around Canterbury, curated by Sandra Drew and featuring work by 22 artists including Phyllida Barlow, Laura Ford and Alison Wilding.

Scottish law rules for the first time that sexual harassment is a form of sex discrimination which can be challenged under the law.

1989

The landmark exhibition *The Other Story* opens at the Hayward Gallery, London. Curated by Rasheed Araeen, the exhibition reflects upon Britain's colonial legacy and highlights the work of post-war Asian, African and Caribbean artists.

1991

Rachel Whiteread is nominated for the Turner Prize. Anish Kapoor wins.

1994

Sense and Sensibility: Women Artists and Minimalism in the Nineties opens at MOMA in New York, featuring major installations and sculptures by seven women artists: Polly Apfelbaum, Mona Hatoum, Rachel Lachowicz, Jac Leirner, Claudia Matzko, Rachel Whiteread and Andrea Zittel.

Shirazeh Houshiary is the first woman of colour to be nominated for the Turner Prize. Antony Gormley wins.

1996

International feminist art journal *n.paradoxa* is founded.

Groundbreaking artist Helen Chadwick dies aged 42.

1997

The Turner Prize sees its first and so far only all-female shortlist, which includes Christine Borland, Angela Bulloch, Cornelia Parker and winner Gillian Wearing.

Rachel Whiteread represents Britain at the Venice Biennale.

1999

Tracey Emin is nominated for the Turner Prize. Her work *My Bed* (1998) causes public controversy and attracts media attention, turning her into a public figure as well as an artist. Steve McQueen wins.

The Sex Discrimination (Gender Reassignment) Regulations make it illegal for employers to discriminate against trans people.

2006

Rachel Whiteread is appointed CBE.

2010

Lubaina Himid is appointed MBE.

Cornelia Parker is appointed OBE.

2011

The Hepworth Wakefield opens. This major art gallery is named after Barbara Hepworth, who was born and educated in the city.

Modern British Sculpture, the first major exhibition to explore the subject in 30 years, opens at the Royal Academy in London. Despite its wide selection of 119 works, only 11 women are represented.

2014

Shared parental leave is introduced, giving a mother the right to transfer periods of leave to a father.

2017

Gillian Wearing's statue of suffragist Millicent Fawcett becomes the first monument in Parliament Square to commemorate a woman or to be created by a woman. It is commissioned to mark the centenary of the 1918 Representation of the People Act, which gave some women over the age of 30 the right to vote.

Phyllida Barlow represents Britain at the Venice Biennale.

Emma Hart becomes the sixth winner of the Max Mara Prize for Women, a collaboration between the Whitechapel Gallery and the Collezione Maramotti, Reggio, Italy.

Lubaina Himid becomes the first woman of colour to win the Turner Prize.

The #MeToo movement against sexual harassment and assault spreads virally online.

2000

Tate Modern opens. Louise Bourgeois is commissioned to create a sculptural work for the Turbine Hall's inaugural display, *Maman* (1999).

2003

2005

Sokari Douglas Camp is appointed CBE.

2015

Sarah Lucas represents Britain at the Venice Biennale.

Maria Balshaw becomes the first female Director of Tate following a successful joint directorship of the Whitworth Art Gallery and Manchester Art Gallery.

Phyllida Barlow is appointed CBE.

2016

Helen Marten wins The Hepworth Wakefield's inaugural Hepworth Prize for Sculpture, for which Phyllida Barlow is also nominated. Marten also wins the Turner Prize.

Revolution in the Making: Abstract Sculpture by Women, 1947–2016, the first major survey on the topic, opens at Hauser & Wirth, Los Angeles, exhibiting nearly 100 works by 34 artists – including British artists Phyllida Barlow and Karla Black.

2018

Veronica Ryan wins the third Freelands Award, resulting in a monographic exhibition at Spike Island, Bristol, in autumn 2020.

Lubaina Himid has her MBE upgraded to a CBE.

Mona Hatoum loses out to Cerith Wyn Evans in the second Hepworth Prize for Sculpture but wins the People's Choice Award.

2019

Cathy Wilkes represents Britain at the Venice Biennale.

Leeds Arts University launches *Feminist Public Sculpture: Championing Women's Achievements in Leeds,* a project aiming not only to commemorate the success of women in the city but also to readdress the gender balance in public sculpture.

Rachel Whiteread has her CBE upgraded to a DBE.

Alison Wilding is appointed OBE.

LIST OF WORKS

All works are Arts Council
Collection, Southbank
Centre, London.

Measurements are given in
centimetres, height x width
x depth.

Not all works may be shown
at all venues.

Anthea Alley
Rock, 1964
Steel
30.5 x 50.8 x 50.8
Purchased 1964
p. 55

Phyllida Barlow
untitled: dunce, 2015
Timber, polystyrene,
paint, paper, wire mesh,
cement, plaster, scrim,
polyurethane foam,
plywood, bonding plaster
310 x 290 x 320
Purchased 2016
p. 51

Rana Begum
No. 429 SFold, 2013
Paint on mirror finish steel
55 x 62 x 19
Purchased 2016
p. 70

Helen Chadwick
*Ego Geometria Sum VIII:
The Horse age 11*, 1982–83
Wood and silver magic
57.5 x 101.9 x 61.9
Purchased 1983
p. 35

Alice Channer
*Maxi, Mini, Midi, Midi, Midi
(Mauve and Cream)*, 2012
Cast and powder-coated
aluminium, oak dowels
70 x 38 x 47
Purchased 2013
p. 42

Lygia Clark
Animal 3, 1969
Aluminium
25 x 35 x 30
Purchased 1970
p. 93

Shelagh Cluett
Light of My Life, 1984
Painted and gilded
aluminium, copper
25 x 14.3 x 5
Purchased 2019

Shelagh Cluett
Untitled, c.1981
Metal
25 x 45 x 10
Purchased 2019
p. 84

Susan Collis
Untitled (rawl plugs), 2007
Brown goldstone and onyx
2 parts, each 0.8 diameter
Purchased 2008
p. 50

Susan Collis
Untitled (rawl plugs), 2007
Brown goldstone and onyx
2 parts, each 0.8 diameter
Purchased 2008
p. 50

Jane Coyle
Peg, 1966
Bronzed metal
36.8 x 32.4 x 19
Purchased 1966
p. 42

Katie Cuddon
A Problem of Departure,
2013
Painted ceramic, pillow
64 x 43 x 30
Purchased 2019
p. 67

Sokari Douglas Camp
Audience (from *Show Boat,
Alali Aru* installation), 1986
Steel
Dimensions variable
Purchased 1988
p. 97

Rose Finn-Kelcey
God's Bog, 2001
Jesmonite,
polypropylene, paint
45.7 x 43.2 x 40.6
Purchased 2019
p. 90

Jessie Flood-Paddock
Snack 16, 2015
Silk, dip-dyed cotton,
epoxy resin, jute,
Jesmonite, spray paint
39 x 23 x 22
Purchased 2019
p. 50

Jessie Flood-Paddock
Snack 20, 2015
Dip-dyed cotton, epoxy
resin, Jesmonite, spray paint
39 x 24 x 24
Purchased 2019

Elisabeth Frink
Head, 1959
Bronze
27.3 x 41.3 x 18.4
Purchased 1959
p. 83

Anya Gallaccio
*can love remember the
question and the answer*, 2003
Mahogany, glass and flowers
275 x 143 x 6
Purchased 2005
p. 63

Katherine Gili
Pistil, 1979
Steel
71.1 x 76.2 x 48.3
Purchased 1979
p. 84

Anthea Hamilton
Leg Chair (Jane Birkin), 2011
Acrylic, brass, photographic
reproductions, 7" single
cover, nylon stockings, wax
81 x 92 x 46
Purchased 2014
p. 69

Mona Hatoum
+ and -, 1994
Wood, metal and sand
8 x 30 x 30
Purchased 1994
p. 49

Jann Haworth
Calendula's Cloak, 1967
Cloth
172.7 x 116.8 x 116.8
Purchased 1969
p. 29

Holly Hendry
*Gut Feelings
(Stromatolith)*, 2016
Plaster, steel, aluminium,
cement, marble, Jesmonite,
birch plywood, pigment, rock
salt, soap, rawhide dog chew
170 x 225 x 100.5
Purchased 2018
p. 39

Barbara Hepworth
Reconstruction, 1947
Oil and pencil on board
34.3 x 46.4
Purchased 1947
p. 26

Barbara Hepworth
Icon, 1957
Wood
49 x 37 x 30
Purchased 1958
p. 56

Shirazeh Houshiary
*Listen to the Tale of the
Reed No. 3*, 1982
Clay and straw on wood
110.5 x 86 x 130
Purchased 1982
p. 82

Karin Jonzen
Seated Nude, 1951
Terracotta
61 x 89.5 x 36
Purchased 1951
p. 27

Permindar Kaur
Innocence, 1993
Cotton and iron
60 x 72cm
Purchased 1996
p. 99

Mary Kelly
*Post-Partum Document,
Documentation VI:
Pre-Writing Alphabet,
Exerque and Diary/
Experimentum Mentis VI:
(On the Insistence of the
Letter)*, 1978–79
Slate and resin
18 parts, each
36.5 x 29 x 4
Purchased 1981
p. 34

Liliane Lijn
See Thru Koan, 1969
Fibreglass, perspex
and motor
112 x 41.5 x 41.5
Purchased 1975
p. 48

Kim Lim
Samurai, 1961
Wood
104.8 x 66 x 60.3
Purchased 1962
p. 28

Gillian Lowndes
Untitled, 1976
Rolled clay dipped
in porcelain slip
19 x 33 x 33
Purchased 2018
p. 55

Sarah Lucas
NUD CYCLADIC 7, 2010
Tights, fluff, wire
Sculpture 47 x 44 x 39
Plinth 121.5 x 43 x 43
Purchased 2012 with the
assistance of the Arts Fund
p. 41

Helen Marten
Bluebutter Idles, 2014
Welded powder-coated
steel, stitched fabric,
french-polished cherry wood,
Valchromat, airbrushed steel,
hand-embroidered fabric,
cast bronze, wicker, cast
plaster, woven straw, leather,
fired clay, shell, butter,
rubber petal
140 x 120 x 83
Purchased 2014 with the
assistance of the Arts Fund
p. 62

Mary Martin
Rotation, 1966
Polystyrene and mirror
9 x 13 x 13
Purchased 1970
p. 49

Cathy De Monchaux
Ferment, 1988
Lead, velvet and steel
24 x 168 x 16
Purchased 1988
p. 33

Lucia Nogueira
One and Three, 1994
Glass, mercury, phosphorus,
paint, and platinum
5.2 x 1 x 1.8
Purchased 1994
p. 98

Margaret Organ
Loop, 1978/2014
Paper, wire, string
197.5 x 144 x 36
Purchased 2016
p. 85

Emma Park
*4 Sculptures 'Untitled
December 1978'*, 1978
Wood
111.5 x 172 x 11
Purchased 1980
p. 75

Cornelia Parker
Fleeting Monument, 1985
Lead, wire and brass
76 x 214 x 214
Purchased 1986
p. 91

Amalia Pica
*Catachresis #40 (teeth
of the rake, leg of the
chair, leg of the table,
head of the screw)*, 2013
Found materials
147.5 x 60 x 60
Purchased 2017
p. 43

Kathy Prendergast
Hair Bonnet, 1997
Human hair
13 x 20 x 20
Purchased 1997
p. 33

Eva Rothschild
Your Weakness, 2004
Ebony, oak and paint
61 x 118 x 63
Purchased 2004
p. 71

Meg Rutherford
Quartros, 1960
Bronze
8.3 x 33 x 20.3
Purchased 1961
p. 93

Veronica Ryan
Territorial, 1986
Plaster and bronze
40 x 219.7 x 147.5
Purchased 1987
p. 57

Grace Schwindt
Position, 2018
Bronze
17 x 15 x 31
Purchased 2019
p. 67

Wendy Taylor
Inversion, 1970
Steel, lacquer and aluminium
89.2 x 275 x 95.3
Purchased 1970
p. 92

Hayley Tompkins
Chair, 2011
Watercolour on wood
79 x 48 x 43
Purchased 2019
p. 61

Shelagh Wakely
Sine Qua Non, 1982
Brass
4 x 27 x 35
Purchased 1983
p. 98

Rebecca Warren
Regine, 2007
Bronze
126 x 37 x 39
Purchased in 2007, with
funds from the McLaren Art
Foundation, in association
with Outset.
p. 40

Rachel Whiteread
Untitled (6 Spaces), 1994
Resin
40 x 313 x 41.5
Purchased 1995
p. 77

Alison Wilding
Untitled, 1980
Zinc and brass
24 x 131 x 160.5
Purchased 1980
p. 76

Rosemary Young
Girl Drying Her Foot,
undated
Bronze
42.5 x 18 x 15.2
Purchased 1955
p. 68

COPYRIGHT CREDITS

The publisher has made every effort to contact all copyright holders. If proper acknowledgement has not been made, we ask copyright holders to contact the publisher. All works are © the artist unless otherwise stated: © Bowness p. 4, p. 26 and p. 56; © the artist's estate p. 27; © Estate of Kim Lim p. 28; © Estate of Helen Chadwick p. 35; © Mona Hatoum p. 49; © Estate of Mary Martin p. 49; © Estate of Gillian Lowndes p. 55; © Estate of Anthea Alley p. 55; © Anya Gallaccio p. 63; © the artist's estate p. 68; © Estate of Elisabeth Frink p. 83; © O Mundo de Lygia Clark-Associação Cultural, Rio de Janeiro p. 93; © Estate of Lucia Nogueira p. 98; © Estate of Shelagh Wakely p. 98; © Permindar Kaur p. 99.

IMAGE CREDITS

All images are courtesy the artist and Arts Council Collection, Southbank Centre, London, unless otherwise stated: photo: Val Wilmer p. 4; Courtesy Carl Freedman Gallery p. 50; Courtesy the artist, Hauser & Wirth and The Fruitmarket Gallery, (photo: Ruth Clark) p. 51; Courtesy the Shelagh Cluett Trust and greengrassi, London (photo: Marcus Leith) p. 84; Courtesy the artist (photo: Nick Singleton) p. 86.

Published on the occasion of the Arts Council Collection exhibition:

Breaking the Mould: Sculpture by Women Since 1945

Longside Gallery, Yorkshire Sculpture Park
4 April – 14 June 2020

The New Art Gallery Walsall
3 July – 6 September 2020

The Levinsky Gallery, The Arts Institute, University of Plymouth
25 September 2020 – 23 January 2021

Djanogly Gallery, Lakeside Arts, University of Nottingham
27 March – 20 June 2021

Ferens Art Gallery, Hull
3 July – 3 October 2021

Exhibition curated by Natalie Rudd, assisted by Laura Biddle

Breaking the Mould is an Arts Council Collection Touring Exhibition initiated in response to *Women Working in Sculpture from 1960 to the Present Day: Towards a New Lexicon*, a research project led by Catherine George (University of Coventry) and Hilary Gresty (independent).

This exhibition has been made possible by the provision of insurance through the Government Indemnity Scheme. Hayward Gallery would like to thank HM Government for providing Government Indemnity and the Department for Culture, Media and Sport and Arts Council England for arranging the indemnity.

Published in 2020 by:
Hayward Gallery Publishing
Southbank Centre,
Belvedere Road,
London SE1 8XX
southbankcentre.co.uk

Art Publisher: Alice Nightingale
Publishing Project Manager: Diana Adell
Sales Manager: Alex Glen
Catalogue design: kellybarrow.co.uk + narratestudio.co.uk
Printed in Ghent by Graphius

Chronology created by Laura Biddle
© Southbank Centre 2020
Texts © the authors 2020
Artworks © the artists 2020 (unless otherwise stated)

A catalogue record for this book is available from the British Library.

ISBN 978-1-85332-367-6

This catalogue is not intended to be used for authentication or related purposes. The Southbank Board Limited accepts no liability for any errors or omissions that the catalogue may inadvertently contain.

Distributed in North America, Central America and South America by:
ARTBOOK | D.A.P.
75 Broad Street, Suite 630,
New York, NY 10004
tel: +1 212 627 1999
artbook.com

Distributed in the UK and Europe by:
Cornerhouse Publications
HOME, 2 Tony Wilson Place,
Manchester, M15 4FN
tel: +44 (0)161 212 3466
cornerhousepublications.org

Cover image: Grace Schwindt, *Position*, 2018
p. 4: Barbara Hepworth in the Palais de Dance studio, St Ives, in 1963 with unfinished wood carving *Hollow Form with White Interior*

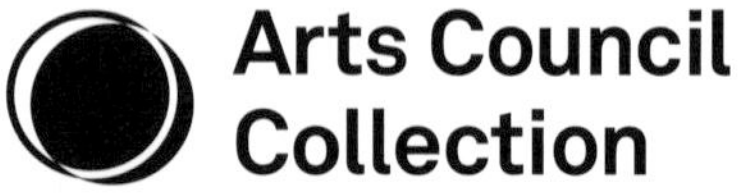

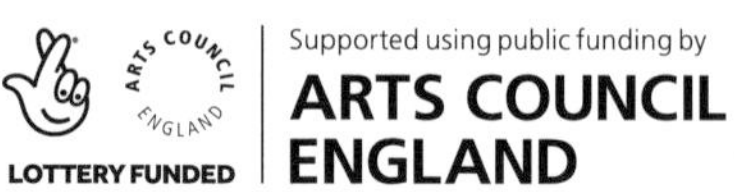